This personalized copy of

The

GOLF GODS

ARE LAUGHING

By Robert Bruce Woodcox

Is printed

Compliments of

PINC Insurance Services

At our 6th annual golf tournament and benefit for the GAI and the PIA Executive Development Program held at Cinnabar Hills Golf Club Monday May 1, 2000

[signature]

Personalized Publis.
By DeHART's Printing Services C
888-982-4POD 408-969-2327 (fax) *www. 7*   *....blishing.com*

PINC Education Foundation

Officially formed in March, 1995, the Foundation's purpose is to provide funding to attract and train new talent to our industry as well as improve the skills of our existing workforce.

The Foundation is made up of three funds, which currently totals over $75,000:

> The Ben Harris Memorial fund
> The Bruce Hart Memorial fund
> The J. Curtis Taylor fund

This annual golf tournament and various fundraising events throughout the year support the general fund.

The Foundation funds provide the following:

> Annual scholarship to the Printing Industries of America's Executive Development Program
>
> Annual scholarship to the National Association of Printers and Lithographers Management Training Institute
>
> Scholarships to the Graphic Arts Institute, four times a year.
>
> Funding for the Career Awareness program

On behalf of the Printing Industries of Northern California, we thank you for your participation and support.

The
GOLF GODS
ARE LAUGHING

The
GOLF GODS
ARE LAUGHING

The Confessions, Obsessions and Insights of a Golf Addict

Robert Bruce Woodcox

SEVEN LOCKS PRESS

Santa Ana, California
Minneapolis, Minnesota
Washington D.C.

Printed in the United States of America

Library of Congress Cataloging-in-Publication Data:

Woodcox, Robert Bruce, 1948-

    The golf gods are laughing / by Robert Woodcox : illustrations by

    Jay Kenton Manning.

    p. cm.

    ISBN 0-929765-65-6

    1. Golf—United States—Humor. I. Title.

GV967.W73   1999   99-20569

796.352'0973—dc21   CIP

Published by Seven Locks Press

PO Box 25689

Santa Ana, California 92799

(800) 354-5348

DEDICATION

To my daughter Jennifer

TABLE OF CONTENTS

ACKNOWLEDGMENTS

This book would not have been written if not for the encouragement of my mother, Marilyn, who started the whole sequence of events that led to the writing of it. Back in 1997 I asked her, "What would you like to do this Mother's Day? She answered, "Let's go play putt-putt golf; I'm tired of buffets."

As we putted those old worn-out balls with those funny rubber-headed fluorescent green and orange putters, she laughed as I told her my golf stories. "Your stories are a riot, Robert. You ought to write a book about them," she encouraged. Her comment planted the seed that grew into this book.

I thank my daughter, Jennifer, whom I love dearly and who is lucky that I didn't discover golf until she was all grown up. Otherwise I might not have known her as well as I do.

My thanks also go to Darlene, who patiently listened to all my stories and every new piece of boring golf information I had to share with her before, during, and after each round.

My teacher Keith Behrens, who helped preserve my sanity, gave me perspective and contributed to the research for this book. And all my friends and golf buddies who inspired me, shared tall tales, and managed not to laugh when I was playing, I thank you also. They included Richard Rakes, Jay Manning, Wes Morrissey, Shawn Cassidy, Richard Klopfstein, Rob MacDonald, and Terry Harmer.

I also want to thank my good friend Jay Manning for allowing me to use his story, "The Legend of a Golf God," in my book.

And last, but by no means least, I must acknowledge my four-legged, best friend, Inkum, who gave up many walks, runs, and other fun things, while I was writing about the game. Thank you, all.

INTRODUCTION

What is the most serious affliction facing American males today—one that encourages shiftlessness, promotes the neglect of business, and eats away at bank accounts? What scourge drives wedges between husbands and wives and causes men to routinely cry? It's golf, or flog, if you spell it backwards, which is a more appropriate name. I began to play the game in my late forties and, viewing myself as a coordinated and athletic individual, felt sure I could play it with relative ease. I was in for a painful surprise.

First of all, golf is not a sport. If it were, all those 67-year-old pot-bellied, one-pack-of-smokes-per-round, arthritic strangers in your foursome would not be shooting 78s while you were throwing clubs at trees because your lean, athletic self couldn't break 100. And further, sports require uniforms. As far as I'm concerned, it's not a sport if you can go out to dinner at a decent restaurant wearing the same clothes you played in all day. No, golf is a game, and like most it demands more of your brain than your body and certainly a good measure of luck to boot. I did not find myself playing it with ease. As a matter of fact, it was excruciatingly difficult.

More than anything, golf requires faith and confidence, neither of which I possessed when I began to play. Now, several years later, having thrown and bent more than my fair share of clubs and cursed the golf gods one too many times, I've made peace with my game. It wasn't easy, but as I started laughing instead of swearing, my game began to improve.

Once I learned not to expect a good round every time out, or even more than once a year, my eyes were opened to the humor of the game and the many ways that it mirrored my attitude about life. As people too often say, "The game is a metaphor for life." And it's true, both are greatly influenced by luck and honesty. The one irrefutable rule of golf that lies at the heart and core of the game is that you must play the ball where it comes to rest, with precious few exceptions. Where it comes to rest is the result of how well or poorly you hit it and, to a great degree, luck. Likewise, how you handle the unfortunate lies of golf and the circumstances of life are what determine your character. Golf is not fair. Life is not fair.

As an example, in the 1998 U.S. Open held at The Olympic Club in San Francisco, California, Payne Stewart enjoyed a flawless first three rounds of golf, playing almost perfectly and maintaining his lead throughout the entire first 54 holes. On the 12th hole of the last round he hit an impeccable drive straight down the fairway. He could not have been in a better position for his approach shot with the exception of one small problem: his ball had come to rest in a sand-filled divot.

Sadly for Stewart, many other players had been hitting to the same area riddling the fairway with divots. In professional tournaments, there isn't enough time between players to replace these, so the officials just fill them with sand and seed.

Stewart's ball was neither a bunker nor a fairway shot. It just wasn't fair. We're supposed to be rewarded for great shots, not punished. Although Stewart had been ahead of the field by as much as 5 strokes over the previous three rounds, he now found himself clinging to a precarious one-shot lead over Lee Janzen, who was ahead of him on the 13th.

The rest of this story is history. Stewart's shot out of the divot strayed right and landed in a bunker. He lost a stroke on the hole and went on to lose to Janzen by 1 stroke, not only a heartbreaking finish but an expensive one: Stewart lost more than $200,000 and a fair amount of pride as runner-up.

I know that as Stewart approached his ball and found it in that little grave, he was already halfway through a prayer to the golf gods for intervention because he knew he wasn't going to get any from the officials (although he did ask). Regardless of his bad luck, he knew he was going to have to play the ball from its sandy lie. On any given day, the only difference between who wins and who places on the PGA (Professional Golfers' Association of America) Tour can be determined by nothing more than a bit of bad luck.

In the 3 years I've been playing, I've stopped throwing clubs and have learned to tone down my language. Having gone from scores in the 130s to a handicap of 11 in less than 2 years, I figured I had conquered both the physical and psychological aspects of the game, but of course I hadn't. In fact, even as my play got better and more consistent my volatility rose to the point where, during one memorable round, I punched a ball-washing machine and broke my hand. This took me out of the game for 12 weeks and was as painful mentally as physically. The frustration of not being able to pursue my passion for more than 3 months was one of the watershed marks in my golf journey. And that's just what it is, a journey, not a destination. We never conquer it. We can't even figure it out. We just try to play as long as we can.

As I began my self-inflicted golf hiatus and my hand started the healing process, so did my brain. It became clear that I was taking the game entirely too seriously. There I was, in a cast, unable to play or write, all because of this silly game. My anger turned to humor and, finally, to an understanding of the game I had not previously possessed.

When I was finally able to write again, I couldn't wait to record on paper all the hilarious situations, incongruities, and incredible stories that had been and would continue to be a part of my golf odyssey. I began asking strangers in my foursomes what their most memorable golf moments were, why they loved and hated the game, and why they kept coming back one miserable round after another. These stories and my own perceptions came to form this book. To paraphrase an old saying, "Those who play well, play. Those that don't, teach. Those that can't do either, write about it."

I firmly believe that even though we may play the game with honesty to a fault, our performance will always depend on three things: luck, the whims of the golf gods, and our sense of humor.

Remember that each time we play, we're using the playground of the golf gods only temporarily, so we have to follow their rules. If we don't, we're punished severely with impossible lies, bad luck, and an incurable slice; and even if we do follow all their rules, we still get punished occasionally, just to remind us we're human.

The Golf Gods Are Laughing is my story and this is my promise: You will laugh, you will be entertained, and you will be informed. What more could you ask of a book or a game? Have fun. May you laugh, have big drives, and 1 putts all day.

THE TEN COMMANDMENTS
ACCORDING TO THE GOLF GODS

Thou shalt always play the ball as it lies.

Thou shalt play the course as thou findest it.

Thou shalt neither take nor give any gimmies.

Thou shalt always post thy true score.

Thou shalt never mix plaids and stripes.

Thou shalt not covet thy partner's driver.

Thou shalt always rake thy bunker after thee.

Thou shalt not kill the ball, unless it's off the tee.

Thou shalt always obey the marshal.

Thou shalt not spend more than three minutes looking
for thy ball, nor wade into water for any reason.

— CHAPTER 1 —

THE QUEST FOR THE PERFECT DRIVER
AND OTHER EQUIPMENT ANXIETIES

The Marquis de Sade Lives in My Garage

I have several torture devices in my garage known as "golf teaching aids." I am the king of golf consumers. When I first began to play, like everyone else I wanted to be good at it. If the latest teaching/torture device promised it would forever rid me of my slice, I would strap it on and hang upside down from the garage rafters every night while listening to self-help tapes and simultaneously chanting golf mantras.

As a result of collecting these gadgets, my garage now looks like the Marquis de Sade's workout room. Among many other strange-looking devices, I have black leather and plastic contraptions to hold my knees together, a Spandex gizmo to squeeze my elbows toward each other, and a hook that's supposed to anchor in my crotch with a length of cord attached to a skullcap to hold my head down. In addition, I have a huge 5-by-6-foot mirror on one wall to watch my backswing. If you walked in there, what would you think?

Also in my garage are at least 35 various clubs that I've purchased and don't use. Eighteen of these are drivers, the other 17 are putters. Drivers and putters are unique among all the other clubs. Although instructors tell us we only have one swing for all our clubs, *we* know better. The driver and the putter are the two most difficult clubs to use. One is the shortest, the other the longest, and both probably account for most of the profits that manufacturers enjoy. These are the two clubs we tinker with and change most often in our futile attempt to make our game better.

With the driver, distance is the goal. Length would seem to be only a male concern. I haven't played golf with many women, so I must admit that I don't have the inside track on this but my girlfriend assures me that length is just as important to the women. I'm talking about the distance we hit the ball off the tee.

Everyone wants to hit it long. For this reason, garages all over the country are strewn with unwanted clubs and golf torture devices guaranteed to lead you to the Holy Grail of distance and proficiency. This would not be the case if we just accepted the fact that the problem isn't with the arrow but with the archer. In our hearts, we know this; we just choose to ignore it, falling prey to every new marketing promise of more distance and better golf.

No matter how much finesse we've developed in the rest of our game, we always want more length off the tee. If we can hit a ball 225 yards, then we want 250. Believe me, even John Daly wants to hit it farther. If he could drive it right up to the green on a par 5, he would. How many golfers do you know who spend the same amount of time practicing their putting as they do their driving? The joy of hitting the ball a very long way off the tee is, in my humble opinion, unequaled in any other sport, with the possible exception of smacking a home run in baseball.

When golf was invented, around 1450, players used gnarly sticks with knots of wood at one end, and the ball was made of wood (later to become a leather orb stuffed with boiled feathers—and *we* think it's hard to get the ball in the hole!). The driver wasn't even invented for another 300 years.

Today, drivers are made of space-age materials found only on other planets. Why else would a single club cost $600? Graphite shafts are so long now they hardly fit into your bag! They hardly fit into a Suburban—even with all the seats down! Heads made of titanium, alpha miraging tri-metals, and kryptonite, are as big as Sunday's meat loaf—all in the name of distance. If a club maker were to manufacture a driver that was 10 feet long, made of pure plutonium, with a head as big as the engine block in your dad's old Chrysler, and promise that the average golfer would get an extra 20 yards off the tee, the club would be back ordered for a year.

Let's take a quick look at what tools our golfing forefathers had to contend with. At the time of King James I of Scotland, clubs were made entirely of wood—shafts were ash or hazel and the head was beech, apple, or pear. If you got hungry during a round, you could eat one. The lie was flatter and the heads much longer than today's clubs. Wooden clubs had quaint names like playclub, brassie, grassed driver, long spoon, and bathie.

In those days, the irons were used only for difficult shots. Considering that golfers played with balls made out of leather stuffed with wet bird feathers, they probably played their irons a lot. Over the years, irons grew to become the club of choice for general approach play. These clubs had names like cleek, niblick, and mashie. Now we have normal names like the *Greatest Big Bertha*™, the *bumble bee whip,* and the *intimidator.* My point is, people had a hell of a good time playing golf back then with the barest of necessities—a stick and a ball full of feathers. Of course no one broke 100 until 1834 either!

Today there are so many pieces of equipment that might be necessary that when you go golfing you pack your bag like you're going into the wilderness for a 2-month camping trip. The bag we are all accustomed to carrying didn't come into existence until 1870. Until that time everyone just lugged their clubs around under their arms. Players put a few balls in their pockets and off they went.

I don't know who invented the golf bag, but it sure was a good idea. At the very least, it gives me a place to put the 25 balls I lose each round. You would think one bag in a few different colors would be sufficient, but now we have so many choices it boggles the mind. There are at least five categories of bags, not to mention hundreds of different colors and a variety of materials—vinyl, canvas, leather, and cotton—to choose from. There are divider bags, drainpipe carry bags, light carry bags, bags with pop-out legs, tournament bags with big hard bottoms for the caddies to sit on—the list goes on.

Back in the good old days, the golf gods didn't care if their clubs got scuffed; after all, they *were* clubs! Now we enshrine them. Not only do we carry them in giant bags, they're often covered up with rubber or furry protective devices. This has always seemed strange to me. Why do people put protective covers on the very same iron instrument that they slam into the ground at 100 miles per hour (MPH)—because they don't want to scratch it? Simple rubber head covers aren't enough. We have to have cute furry animal heads for our woods. In fact, Tiger Woods has little tigers on his woods.

Packing Your Bag for a Long Trip

While I was writing this, I was reminded of just how big my golf bag is. I stepped away from the computer and went to the garage to look at what was in my bag, other than the obvious clubs and balls. Here is what I found:

There were three pockets I didn't even know I had, so of course, these were empty. All the others, however, were full. I had 19 clubs, 62 balls, and 34 wooden tees. There were two sticks of very old gum, three Q-Tips, two golf receipts, and six Band-aids.

I found not one, but three different spike-mark-repair tools, one of which I remember cost me $23 and is combined with a commemorative ball-marker coin. I've never used it. Twenty-three bucks— what was I thinking?

Then there were two towels and four rumpled business cards (two were mine and two belonged to guys I don't remember). I had a tube of Ben-Gay, a bottle of aspirin, an unmatched pair of short white socks, two old leather gloves that looked like prunes, a yardage gizmo that looks like a surveyor's transit that cost $50 at Sharper Image, an old tassel off a previous golf shoe, and a little booklet with on-the-run quick golf tips.

Hold it! That's not all! There was a stickum note pad, a leaky ball-point pen, an old bag of peanuts and raisins, an empty plastic water bottle, a piece of petrified apple, tubes of 30 and 45 SPF (sun protection factor) sunscreen, a spike remover tool, and my notes on swing thoughts from 1995. In addition there were two types of brushes for cleaning clubs (one was a plastic and wire bristle brush, the other was a bottle with a little brush on top) a raincoat hood and an umbrella, a ball cap, a pair of shoes, and a golf coupon book. There was some loose change and, lo and behold, a $20 bill! I know guys who could survive at the North Pole for 6 months on less.

A Shopping Spree at Golf World

Golf is a $16-billion-a-year industry. According to the National Golf Association, nearly $12 billion of this is spent on green fees, carts, driving ranges and lessons, and about $4 billion is being spent on equipment.

There are fundamental reasons for all this spending: The quest for more distance, the thirst for more accuracy, the hunger for lower scores, and the craving for better putting.

If you've ever listened to a commercial or read an ad for golf equipment, you'll recognize this copy in one form or another: "Do you want to hit it longer, play better, and lower your score? Then you're gonna love this new widget, guaranteed to take 20 strokes off your score on your next round or your money back if you're not 100 percent satisfied." Now read the fine type: *Just pack up all the crap that we sent you in the proper bags and compartments, seal it just like you got it, using the original packing tape, pay $185 in postage to get it back to us, and we'll promptly refund your money.* The only way I know to guarantee shaving 20 strokes off my game would be to quit after 16 holes.

D+A=LS+MFROWIC—*Distance plus accuracy equals lower scores and more fun, regardless of what it costs.* Believe me, I know this formula firsthand. When I first began playing, I spent nearly $10,000 on green fees, lessons, clothes, and equipment and that was just in the first 6 months. If I had purchased stock in "Golf World" when I first started playing, I would be a millionaire by now and the SEC would be investigating me for insider trading, surmising the rise in the stock price came mostly from my own spending at the stores. I've supported one of these huge outlets almost single-handedly, buying driver after driver in my search for one that would deliver the big hit; various wedges that promised me more finesse; and one putter after another, each implying that I would putt straighter than I had before.

The owners of "Golf World" are geniuses. They know I will keep coming back for bigger and better everything. They know I crave the newest and hottest. They know I believe everything I read in those golf magazines and hear on the commercials. Their marketing concept is simple: If a customer doesn't like what he has purchased (e.g., if he can't drive the ball farther and putt straighter), then he can bring it back within 30 days for a full refund. If he keeps the equipment longer than 30 days, he can still bring it back and get a store credit for about 60 percent of the original purchase price. Then, of course, he upgrades from the chintzy $400 driver to the $600 driver. He gets a credit for about $200 and he's ecstatic because, after all, he did use the old club for 6 weeks and is now buying that $600 driver for only $400.

At "Golf World" they let me test the equipment before purchasing, even brand new $600 drivers. The stores have nifty areas where you can hit balls off mats into nets. The only problem with this is that I can't tell where or how far my ball might be going, or if I'm even hitting it well. To be sure I can actually hit with the club, I have to buy it and take it to the course only to once again experience the disappointment that I'm not hitting the ball 285 yards and straight as an arrow. So, back I traipse to Golf World to tell them I don't like the driver. I'm too embarrassed to admit that I can't hit the damn ball, so I mumble that I just don't like the club. In my first year alone, I bought and traded in four complete sets of irons, five or six wedges, four or five putters, and at least five drivers.

The Clubs You Need and the Distance You'll Get with Them

Golfers assemble their own set of clubs best suited to their game. Contrary to popular opinion, the best clubs for you aren't necessarily a matched set from one manufacturer. All my irons match, but my woods are each made by different manufacturers because those are the ones that work for me.

According to the golf gods, we're supposed to carry only 14 clubs. I carry about 29 and a few garden tools just to be sure. After all, I'm not playing in the PGA, so who's going to count? It also helps if I keep fuzzy covers on about 10 of them; then it's harder to tell how many clubs I'm carrying.

Here's what's in my bag: Two drivers (I never know which one I'll be able to hit that day, so one's an offset and the other's a regular). For this same reason, I carry a 2- and 3-wood as alternate drivers. I also carry a 4-, 5-, 7-, 9-, 11- and a 13-wood and my newest: 20-wood! I don't carry any iron longer than an 8, and I have 9 wedges ranging from a standard 48 degrees to my lobbiest lob wedge at 88 degrees. If I can't get that one under the ball, I go to my scythe.

Make sure when you practice that you know without a doubt, how far you hit with each club. Knowing this and making the right club selection every time will take at least 6 strokes off your game. Here is the average distance most of us hit the ball with our various clubs:

The woods:

- Driver   185 yards
- 3-wood   195 yards
- 5-wood   185 yards
- 7-wood   160 yards

The irons:

- 1-iron   Didn't know they made 'em
- 2-iron   Never seen one
- 3-iron   Don't have one
- 4-iron   145 yards
- 5-iron   145 yards
- 6-iron   145 yards
- 7-iron   145 yards
- 8-iron   130 yards
- 9-iron   130 yards
- Wedge   130 yards
- Sand wedge   45 yards

Equipment Tips

Before you buy all those rubber gizmos and swingy things, buy a large mirror and grab an old tire from the dumpster at your local tire store. Affix the mirror to the wall in the garage. Put the tire on the floor and put a sandbag in the center of it, to keep it from moving. Now step up to the tire as if it were the tee and swing the club into the tire while watching your backswing in the mirror. Not only will this help groove your swing, but you'll begin to see what impact looks like. If this doesn't help, you can feel free to spend the money you saved on some lessons and buy some of those torture devices.

— CHAPTER 2 —

GETTING YOUR BALL BEARINGS

The first golf balls were made of wood in the 15th century. By the 16th century these were replaced with the "feathery," a curious orb of leather filled with boiled bird's feathers and then dried and pounded with a mallet into a sort of ball shape. It took a skilled worker a full day to make three of these balls, which made them expensive: a dozen balls cost more than a week's wages for many enthusiastic golfers. Not much has changed in the cost to play the game since then! Despite being expensive, easily damaged, and difficult to make, the feathery remained popular until the 19th century when it evolved into a rubber-like substance known as the *guttie.*

Around 1909, a gentleman named Coburn Haskell, a wealthy American amateur golfer, collaborated with the Goodrich Rubber Company to develop a much livelier ball of rubber thread wound around a solid rubber core. These balls were cheaper than the guttie and they traveled farther off the tee but they were hard to control on the greens. Again, not much has changed in the game since its early days.

Mr. Haskell's prototype was the predecessor of the modern ball. The official USGA (United States Golf Association)—sanctioned golf ball cannot be smaller than 1.68 inches in diameter and it's so important that an entire page of the USGA's 1997 *Rules* book is devoted to it. The rules are so specific they even dictate that the weight not exceed 1.62 ounces. Today, balls are manufactured by dozens of different companies who promise their product will fly higher or lower, longer, or with more spin. There are balls for seniors, balls for women, and different balls for the pros. Then, just when modern technology managed to create round "bullets" capable of astounding accuracy and distance, the USGA stuck its nose in with a ruling that capped the ball's maximum speed at 250 feet per second and a maximum distance of 280 yards (including carry and roll). They must measure this with robotics and computers because there are plenty of pros hitting the ball more than 300 yards.

Why You Shouldn't Lick Your Balls

Your balls are important. Wash them but don't lick them. I used to lick mine before putting to get the grass stains off them. (As if a stain would affect the roll of the ball.) And while we're on the subject, don't chew your tees either. Once your tees and balls have made contact with the turf a few times, they're covered with deadly chemicals, the same substances that kill bugs and keep the grass really green. Most of these chemicals cause birth defects in lab rats. Who knows, maybe they cause golf defects, too.

The best way to clean your balls is to use one of those handy little red or green ball-washing machines found at most course tees for that purpose. If nothing else, it is great fun to pump that contraption up-and-down while you rotate your ball in between the bristles with the handle.

This convenient device is actually called a Par Aide and was invented in 1954 by Joseph Garske, who referred to it as a "spiraling agitator." It's a very functional device, so much so that an entire company was founded upon this one invention. Besides cleaning your ball, it also provides a little distraction while you wait interminably for the group in front of you to move ahead so you can tee off.

The fact is most of us can't drive the ball beyond 210 yards, but we insist on waiting for the group in front of us to move past the 280-yard range, not because we really care if we hit them, but because, who knows, this may be the day we actually drive our ball 250 yards! It may career off a rock in the fairway and take one of those once-in-a-lifetime rolls.

What Are Dimples For?

There is a very important reason for washing your balls other than pure fun. It helps them fly better. Why do balls fly other than the fact that they are being catapulted by a hard metal object moving at about

100 miles an hour? They fly because they have dimples—those ubiquitous little depressions on the surface of the ball—and if your dimples are dirty or filled with muck, you won't get a dynamic ball flight.

Ball makers spend a fortune designing and experimenting with dimples. Depending upon the total number and size of the dimples, your ball will travel vastly different routes, assuming all other factors are equal—the speed of your swing, the humidity in the air, and the club you're using. I guess that's why they're tested with computers and not people, because absolutely nothing about the game is equal when humans swing a club.

Today's balls are designed with a very specific geometric dimple pattern called a *dodecahedron.* For those of you who have been out of high school geometry more than 4 months, a dodecahedron is essentially a 12-sided pentagonal shape with 10 equators, none of which actually touch another. Amazing—all of that is going on around that little 1.68-inch surface.

The essential reason for dimples—and for so many of them—is to give the ball lift and spin, not that all our shots have these essential qualities. It also helps to hit the ball squarely with some hard object. However, in their rush for ever greater distance, trajectory, spin, and sales, the manufacturers are closing in on the ball that will go 290 yards without actually being hit with a club. Whoever achieves this first will be the next Bill Gates of the sports world.

Which Color Is Right for You?

All golfers hit the ball differently and therefore need to use different types of balls. At least that's what the ads want us to believe. There are balata balls, so named because the rubber used to make them comes from balata trees. Unfortunately, because so many people now play golf balata tree has been listed as an endangered species. Fake rubber is now used, but the end products are still called balata balls, nevertheless. These balls are made of rubber strands that are stretched from their original length of about 3 feet to almost a mile long as they are wrapped around the ball's core. All this rubber supposedly makes the ball soft and imparts more "feel" to the player. The balata ball is reputed to be a better ball for use around the greens and for putting than its cousin, the two-piece, high-velocity, long-distance balls, which is harder and better for the long game. Some of these now even have titanium cores!

I'm sorry, but the word "feel" isn't in my golf vocabulary. I've rubbed my balls, rotated them in my hands, and played with them, but I still can't feel one iota of difference between either of them. Personally, I want one thing and one thing only: for my ball to go straight out and onto the fairway as far as it can possibly fly. I don't care if it's a high or low trajectory. I'm not disappointed if it never rises 3 inches above the ground, and I could care less if my ball is more "forgiving" around the green. Just give me *long* and true. I want to be confident that when I clink that little dimpled globe *way* off center, it still has a reasonable chance of reaching the green in 2.

We all want the impossible. That's why we continue to spend billions of dollars on new equipment, all in the near futile attempt to gain distance and accuracy. Manufacturers further compound the confusion by making balls in different colors. My preference is still white, although I do like the bright yellow and orange ones: they're easier to find.

In the final analysis, color doesn't make much difference. I'm convinced that despite all the sophisticated research conducted on golf balls, manufacturers have yet to discover what most of us have theorized all along—balls have minds of their own! I've tested this hypothesis by sneaking up on the ball, hoping to catch it napping, thus mindless for the moment. This doesn't work because as soon as you are aware of the ball, it is aware of you. Think about the last time you stepped up to the tee on a par 3 with water on the left. Knowing you have a tendency to slice, which will be particularly helpful in this instance, you take your standard swing, anticipating the ball will bend right. Of course this time it takes off straight and drowns in the pond.

Ball Hunters

The primary reason it takes so long to play a round of golf these days, other than the fact that there are too many people playing, is "ball hunters." According to the USGA rules, we are only allowed 5 minutes to look for our ball. Even that seems too generous to me. A round of golf is supposed to take about 4 hours. My last outing was 6! We played behind a fivesome that spent most of the day on both sides of the fairway interminably looking for balls. As if it's not bad enough that some people spend half an hour looking for their ball in the rough, they have to get into hip-high waders and use aluminum poles to search for balls in the ponds too! This kind of activity is extremely insensitive, cheap, and aggravating to most golfers, and it takes income away from the people who do it for a living.

Although ball hunters are a loathsome lot, I actually admire one gentleman who seems to have raised ball hunting to an art form and even appears to make a living collecting and selling his treasure. At one of the short executive courses I play to hone my chipping skills (and I use the word "skills" very loosely, because my chipping looks more like tiddlywinks than golf), the 6th hole backs up to a dirt road. A 40-foot length of chain-link fence runs alongside the tee. Every Saturday and Sunday, an old, crumpled guy, who looks like he sleeps under a freeway overpass, sits on a wooden bench on the other side of the fence, attending to hundreds of cellophane-bagged balls he has hanging from the fence. He must have thousands, packaged a dozen to the bag. His wares sell anywhere from $5 to $10 a dozen, depending upon appearance, and he's even enterprising enough to sell soda and candy bars, too. I wondered how he manages to retrieve so many balls, and so one day, when play was backed up, I asked him. This is what he told me:

I get up an hour before sunrise, climb the fence and begin my search. It's not easy you know. There's an art to it, son. You see most golfers either slice or hook, but the majority slice, so I begin on the right side of the fairways. I start out at about 150 yards from the tee because sliced balls roll less than the ones that are hooked. I always start at the first tee because that's where most bad golfers have the worst tee shot of the day and, when they lose one, they won't spend long looking for it because there's always a gaggle of guys impatiently tapping their toes, waiting behind the first tee staring at them. When I'm looking on the right side I always look in the deep stuff, because those sliced balls go real high and when they land they really bury themselves. On the other hand, on the left side I look closer in to the tee because a lot of those balls are heeled so they tend to scoot just under range of radar and get snagged closer to the fairway. Some of my best finds are in the most obvious places, the lowest points of terrain.

I thought to myself, "He's right on the mark. Because balls are round, and objects in motion tend to stay in motion, balls will seek the lowest point of gravity—ravines, gullies, ditches, and the edges of ponds where most people don't even begin to look, always assuming that their ball took a bath, and justifiably so, I might add." I was fascinated with the extent of his knowledge of the game and how he applied his ingenuity to finding balls.

Harry was his name and golf-ball-finding was his game. For all I know, Harry lives in one of the mansions near the course, paid for by many years of ball hunting, and he probably hasn't anything better to do at night anyway.

Diving for Dollars

Ball diving is a multimillion dollar industry. One of the biggest retrieval companies in the country services about 75 courses, and their certified Scuba divers take more than 156,000 balls out of one pond, on one course alone each year. All told, of the approximately 600 million new balls sold each year, more than 200 million of them are scooped out of lakes and ponds.

Ball use and re-use is a vicious cycle. First we buy 600 million balls, then we promptly lose 200 million in the drink. These balls are then cleaned up and, in some cases, repainted, and resold to the clubs at about 10 to 15 cents per ball. The clubs then sell them back to the very same guys who lost them in the first place and spent half an hour holding up play looking for them in order to save a buck.

It would be interesting if there were a way to track how many times these same balls go through this cycle. For all we know, that one-dollar ball could have been retrieved, repainted, and redunked many, many times. This is called "ball reincarnation"—for those balls without a mind of their own.

What intrigues me is this: If every one of us wants to play well and hit the ball long and straight, why would anyone buy a one-dollar ball that is waterlogged and repainted? When a ball is repainted, the dimples change. They aren't as deep as when they had only one coat of paint. This means the recycled ball isn't going to fly as far or as accurately, which, in turn, means that more of them will find their way to the pond again.

Here's something to think about: We know that approximately 600 million new balls are purchased every year and about 200 million are retrieved from the water and resold. But those 200 million water balls do not take into account balls lost on the course, and I'm sure that number is twice as large. During an average round on an average course, I can count on losing at least five balls in the rough and sometimes in grass only 1 inch deep. Where do all these balls go? Do the greenskeepers find them when they trim the rough? Are they scooped up and resold? Or are they like the one sock of a pair, vanished from the dryer without a logical trace? Perhaps they end up in golf heaven and that's what the golf gods play with.

Ball Tips

Here are some bits of ball wisdom:

- Don't be cheap. Buy good balls. Buy the color that goes best with your socks.
- Use a nonerasable laundry pen and mark your balls with a creative design or slogan to avoid fighting with everyone on the course over which "Zingblatt 3" is yours—the one next to you or the identical ball 3 feet away.
- Keep your balls clean. Remember, good clean dimples and plenty of them are the keys to long and straight drives.
- Forget about how many layers your balls have and just buy *big* balls. You can't use them in tournaments, but how many tournaments do you play in? I use the oversized variety. I don't know if I hit them any farther, but psychologically it's just nice to know there's more ball there. After all, the rules only state that the ball *can't be less* than 1.68 inches in diameter. They don't say anything about how *big* it can be.
- Check your bag before you start a round to be sure you have the two dozen balls you'll need to finish the day. It's extremely embarrassing to ask your friends to lend you balls in the middle of a round.
- And last, even though they are expensive, absolutely, under no circumstances should a golfer ever spend more than 3 minutes looking for a ball.

— CHAPTER 3 —

THE ART OF THE DIVOT

The word "divot" is derived from the ancient words of the golf gods, "dive at" (as in, dive at the ground with a B-52 bomber, thereby displacing huge quantities of earth and sod with a heavy metal object).

The divot is a subject unto itself. My golf instructor always tells me, "You must learn to take a divot." Actually, you don't take a divot, you leave one since, technically speaking, the divot is the gorge left in the course by the violent flailing about that we all like to call our swing. Why else would the tools of the game be called clubs? The 4-pound chunk of grass and dirt that flies through the air (taking with it your pride and some yardage) doesn't technically have a name, although I like to think of it as the divot lid.

"Replace your divot" is one of the cardinal rules of the golf gods. This is not an easy task. If your divot is the hole that is left in the ground, you can't technically replace it. You have to fill it with the chunk of earth that flew off somewhere into space. This presents immediate problems. First, you must find your own lid among hundreds of other similar chunks of earth slung into the void by your fellow golfers before you. One clue: the older ones that weren't replaced are usually dry and yellow. The new ones are juicier and still green. Yours is out there somewhere and if you don't replace it, some poor shmuck's ball is going to land in your divot and then he will have to cheat when no one is looking and give it the old "foot wedge" to nudge it out of his impossible lie. Your lie, by the way, is not your score. It's where your ball comes to rest after being hurled incoherently into the cosmos.

Why Marshals Have Jobs

One of the many paradoxes of golf now comes into play: You are simultaneously told to replace your divots and speed up your play! Keeping up with the golfers in front of you is one of the most distracting rules of the game. You will find admonishments on every conceivable printable surface around the course—from harsh warnings on your scorecard to signs posted at every tee. The warning to keep up is everywhere, and if you don't, the golf police will be there to remind you.

As we already discussed, marshals have just two responsibilities: speeding us along and insuring we wear collared shirts. Speeding up while simultaneously stopping to hunt hither and yon for divot lids are not compatible activities. Divot or not, everyone knows that the very nature of golf is agonizingly slow. It's meant to be that way. Golf is part Zen and part masochism—mostly masochism.

Golf Toupees

Divot lids are a sight to behold. They are like miniature flying sod saucers that don't spin off into space as much as they tumble head over heels spewing slabs of tundra as they lurch through the sky and plop to earth somewhere. Most golfers are good at eventually finding theirs and they are equally adept at replacing them. This is proper and important. For if this isn't done, the fairway (and I don't know why they call it "fair" way because it certainly isn't) soon begins to resemble a giant brown cheese grater.

In the California desert communities of Palm Springs, Bermuda Dunes, and Rancho Mirage, if you don't replace or put sand in your divot, you are first given a warning then promptly ejected from the course upon your second lapse of manners.

The now retired tour player Julius Boros, while breaking in a new and very young caddie years ago, told him to pick up a big divot he had just created. As they continued the round, the caddie was reminded to pick up each divot. On the second tee, Boros turned to get a club from the boy and found him standing there holding two huge divot lids—he had never told the caddie to replace them.

A professional golfer's divots are quite different from yours or mine. The major difference is that a professional's divots are in front of where their ball *was*. Ours are mostly behind where the ball still *is*. This is also known as "hitting it fat," "chunking it," or "chili-dipping." The appropriate term depends upon which club you used and how far away you were from the green. If you used a 3-iron, this would be referred to as hitting it fat and would most likely elicit only a moan. Rolling up carpet next to the green with a sand wedge would be grounds for suicide.

How to Become a Better Golfer by Beating Up Mother Nature

It is difficult to determine which is most embarrassing: sculling the ball or taking huge divots before hitting the ball. If you are taking a divot, even if it's before the ball, you're at least beginning to get the right idea.

If you pay attention, you'll notice that divots tell you what you're doing right and wrong. Tour pro Tom Lehman says, "Let your divots be your teacher." This is a smart idea and is also much cheaper than lessons. After you strike your ball look at the divot carefully. Does it aim to the right or left of where your ball traveled? If you are right-handed and it aims to the left, you sliced; if it aims to the right, you hooked it; if it is straight, in all probability your ball flight was too. Try to leave your divots in neat straight lines going the same direction you want your ball to travel.

The only places you shouldn't take a divot are on your drive, with your fairway woods, or when you're putting. In all other cases you want to plunder and pillage the landscape leaving many toupees— proof that you're playing better golf.

How to Avoid Divots

One of the predecessors to the modern game of golf, generally agreed to have begun in Scotland, was the game of kolf or kolven played in Holland. Kolf was played on ice! These guys did not have a problem with divots. They used primitive sticks to hit a rock at posts frozen in the ice. (Kind of a combination of hockey and golf I suppose.) They should've called it "kolfky."

In today's game, however, there is only one true way to avoid leaving a divot. That would be to travel to and play in Dhahran, Saudi Arabia. As you might expect, grass is at a premium on this desert course. In fact, the only reason grass is found on the greens is that the pins don't stand up very well in sand.

Each player is required to carry his own mat or rug to each place his ball comes to rest in the sand. The player is then allowed to pick up the ball and place it on his hitting rug for the next shot. This makes it virtually impossible to leave a divot with the exception of the remote possibility that you might gouge out a portion of the green with your putter and with my game, even that isn't so remote.

A case in point: I once asked a local pro if there was any rule that prohibited me from using a club on the greens other than the putter. To my astonishment, I found out that it is perfectly legal to use any club I wanted, provided I didn't take a divot out of the green. You're probably asking yourself, "Why would I want to use any club on the green other than a putter?" Well, how about the 6th hole at Riviera with the sand trap in the middle of it? Going around it once cost me 4 putts. The next time I played, I used a sand wedge to get over the bunker and only needed 1 putt.

If the worst does happen and you find your ball resting in someone else's small grave, the golf gods don't let you pick it up. You're not even allowed to touch it, you're just out of luck, just as you would be if you had found yourself behind a tree. Remember, you must play your ball where you find it. That's the fun of the game, isn't it? Let's face it, you're probably not going to wind up with a very good shot when your ball gets submerged in one of these crypts. In all likelihood, you will yank it straight up into the air and it will land 3 inches in front of you, while your divot has sailed quite nicely up the fairway 70 yards. So before you take your stance, get down on both knees and pray to the golf gods for forgiveness. You are being punished, probably for not replacing one of your divots somewhere along the line.

This is a good place to introduce one of the golf gods—the big Kahuna himself, Kallowae (he of the extremely long drive!). He's the one who came up with the ridiculous concept of "playing it where it lies." Not everyone believes that the gods meant this in the strictest sense and so some players take little liberties and occasionally use the old foot wedge instead of the sand wedge to extricate their ball before proceeding with their true shot. The modern day rules at least allow us relief from ground that is under repair but even that was not the intent of the gods. Believe me, they meant it literally and in all fairness, I have to agree, for it is this simple rule that makes the game what it is: a test of your character as much as your ability.

The golf gods delight in our obsessing to take control of the game when, in fact, it's the letting go that allows us to play better. It was this very problem of landing in a divot the day I was about to break 100 for the first time that I began to understand the golf gods and why they are laughing. On that day, I made a horrific shot out of a huge divot, thereby ruining my chances to shoot 99. I don't know about you, but to me a 99 feels like 10 strokes less than a 100; likewise, an 89 feels like 10 strokes less than a 90.

Divot Tips

Here are some ways to improve your divot behavior:

- Try to leave a divot on all iron shots. This means hitting your ball first, then taking some sod. Note that the ball should travel much farther than the sod.

- Replace all your divots or put some sand and seed in them to promote good fairways for the next guy, even if the marshal is chasing you to speed up your play.

- Always try to keep your ball in the shortest grass you can find, preferably in the fairway. This makes it easier to leave a divot and it will bring your score down dramatically.

- Plunder and pillage the landscape. Pound Mother Nature into submission with your irons. Just make sure to clean up after yourself.

CHAPTER 4

HANDICAPPING FOR FUN AND PROFIT

Before we all became more sensitive, the physically impaired were referred to as "handicapped." It is no longer polite to use this term except on parking stall signs and at golf courses, where basically everyone is handicapped. To prove it, I give you the USGA's handicapping system, which reminds you just how disabled you really are.

Why We're All Physically Impaired on the Golf Course

Like the game itself, the USGA handicapping system is based on honesty, which is to say that you are trusted to post your own score on the USGA computer system after each game.

Here's how you achieve your handicap. Once you have registered with a USGA-sanctioned golf course or club, every time you play a round of golf, you are trusted to enter your true score for that round and the date into a computer terminal in the pro shop. After you have played 20 rounds of golf, the USGA or your local affiliate—such as the Southern California Golf Association (SCGA)—computes your average score after they take out the highest 10 rounds. The average number of strokes over par for the remaining 10 rounds (in my case it was 20) is your starting handicap. You continue to enter your score after each round, and your handicap is recomputed at the end of each month by dropping the highest 10 scores and averaging the rest of them. It doesn't matter how many rounds you've played that month, your 10 highest scores are deducted.

If it weren't for cheating, the handicapping system would work quite well. Golf is the only game in which amateur players enjoy a level playing field. If my handicap is a 12 and yours is an 18, we can still play together and have great fun and you don't have to attain a score lower than mine to be equal.

If players are posting their real scores, then why do most look like they're at an ATM at midnight, on the bad side of town, withdrawing

$500? Because they don't want anyone else to see the scores they put into the computer, that's why. For the most part, it's only the really good players with big egos who don't cheat.

A friend of mine who's a scratch golfer tells me he can't wait to get to the computer and post his score when he's played a bad game. That's because he wants as many high scores as possible in the system so he'll look worse than he actually is. Then, when he plays in tournaments, he'll be pitted against golfers who really are worse than he is but, at least by the numbers in the computer, he should have an equal chance.

There are three reasons for the system:

- To make the playing field level for everyone—a noble cause.
- To seed people properly for tournaments.
- To give all bettors an even chance at cheating.

As if you didn't already know how difficult the game is, here's further proof: the overall U.S. Average handicap index hasn't gone down in 20 years! The average score for a round of golf is 107. Furthermore, fewer than 100 golfers in the entire world of approximately 50 million players make a good living at it, and fewer than 500 golfers can eke out any existence at all. Of the 50 million players, 1/4 percent play scratch golf. In other words, we are *not* getting any better.

In track and field within the last few decades, the 4-minute mile was broken and the high-jump bar was raised from 5 feet to nearly 8. In baseball, Mark McGwire eclipsed Roger Maris's feat of 61 home runs. And in basketball, Michael Jordan routinely scored 40 points a game. Athletes in just about every conceivable sport have gotten faster, stronger, and smarter, but not in golf. In golf, we just make the equipment faster, stronger, and smarter.

If I were to plot a chart of my own handicap over the past few years, it would look like a blueprint for building a roller coaster. I recorded 132 strokes on my very first game. Within 2 years I had my handicap down to 11. Now it's 17. Just when I think I've got it all figured out and I'm headed toward single digits, presto! I'm right back in the minor leagues.

Courses have handicaps too, depending upon their length and degree of difficulty. Now though, the USGA doesn't think it can handicap them enough to keep up with all the new technology the pros are using. With that in mind, let's take a look at two divergent perspectives on the development and use of all this new equipment.

Bigger and Straighter or Smaller and Shorter—The Argument Rages On

You're probably familiar with the recent argument that's been raging in golf. It centers around the explosion in equipment. I think it began in earnest after Tiger Woods's overwhelming victory at the 1997 Masters in Augusta. Manufacturers know golfers will always buy the latest and greatest in their quest for farther and straighter drives, so we can hardly blame them for creating better and better equipment. Or can we?

One side of the argument goes this way: There is a glut of high-flying technology. In 1996, John Daly was averaging 305 yards per drive. I have a neighbor who is a diabetic, has one kidney, is 63 years old, is very skinny, and has a horrible swing; and he hits the ball 275 yards with his kryptonite driver! Is this fair?

Many advocates of the old way argue that our golf courses are becoming easy bombing runs for pros using plutonium drivers and technologically advanced balls, when they're in the hands of the pros. Tee shots whiz by old fairway bunkers as if they were mere landscape decorations, and new titanium-centered balls need parachutes for re-entry. So let all the weekend players have their fun and drive the ball 300 yards, but let's see the USGA let some air out of the ball and take some impact out of the clubs. After all, in professional baseball they still use wooden bats and the ball is still sheathed in leather with knotted stitching, and the National Football League ball has remained unchanged for 60 years. So why do the USGA and the PGA allow the use of 22nd-century technology now?

On the other side of the argument are the futurists who ask, How can we open that bag of tees?—a different standard for amateurs and professionals. One of the thrills of the game for the weekend player is the ability to hit the occasional shot as well as a pro. You can't play one-on-one with Shaquille O'Neal but, with your new titanium driver, you can hit it as far as some of the pros once in awhile, and you can certainly get lucky occasionally and sink a long putt as well as the big boys.

If you want to put some punch back into the professional game, put some really hard sand—and plenty of it—in the bunkers and then water them down the morning of the tournament. While you're at it, let the fairway grass grow higher than a 1/4 inch. Today's tour fairways are cut so low and maintained so firmly that a pro can get an extra 45 yards of roll out of a drive.

Let the pros play under the same conditions as the weekend players: on fairways that feature wagon wheel ruts, bunkers of wet compacted dirt, unrepaired divots the size of moon craters, and plenty of bald spots. We survived the era of wooden balls and hickory shafts. We'll survive titanium.

Reader, you make your own decisions. Myself? I carry 29 clubs in my bag and a few assorted gardening tools. I don't play in tournaments and I rarely gamble. I just want a low score. Let the amateurs play with whatever equipment they can buy or invent and slow down the pros with a different ball. After all, in many sports the equipment is different for the college and pro players. The college football is smaller than that used in the professional game; the three-point line in collegiate basketball is closer to the basket than in the pros; and the aluminum bats used in college are outlawed in the big leagues.

Handicapping Tips

Here are a few reminders of how handicaps can work for you:

- If you have a high handicap, take heart. Look at it this way: If you're paying an average of $100 a round on a nice public course and you shoot 120 and you're playing with a friend who shoots a 75, who got the most for their money? You did! At $100 for 120 strokes you only paid 83 cents per hack. Your partner, on the other hand, paid almost $1.33.

- Further, take heart. If you have a high handicap and you are fortunate enough to play and bet against an opponent who has given himself a "vanity" handicap, you will be able to take home some serious money. What is a vanity handicap? Some people actually cheat the other way; they put scores into the computer that are far lower than their true numbers. They go completely foggy when it comes to remembering those mulligans and foot wedges. This kind of person would rather appear to be a good golfer than actually be one. He's like the guy who goes to the ski resort with a fake leg cast on. Unfortunately, it is difficult to find any of these types that will wager. Think of it this way: Do you actually believe that Bill Clinton's handicap is a 12?

— CHAPTER 5 —

THE INCREDIBLE SHRINKING HOLE

Why There Are Only 18 Holes

Although historical footnotes document May 14, 1754, as the day that 22 gentlemen formed the Society of St. Andrews Golfers and decreed that 18 holes should constitute a round, no one was quite sure why that number was chosen until recently.

Thanks to the good folks at Macallan, makers of a particularly good single-malt scotch, for recently offering this explanation:

> The Truth. The 18-hole truth…In 1858 whin my granfaythir was playin' at dear ould St. Andra', there cam' a day whin the club decided that the number o' holes on courses shud be standardized. But the cummittee chosen tae determine the matter couldna' cum tae a meetn' o' minds. Then granfaythir spoke up.
>
> "As ye ken," he said, "the winds are often raw hereaboot. As ye nae doot do, I carry wi' me a gill o'whiskey ta waarm ma bones. I use a sml glass which huds exactly an oonce an' a hoff. As lang as the gill lasts, I find it pleasant ta continue ma gam' o' golf. When the bottul's empty, it wud be foo' hardy indeed ta do so. I hae fund that bottul will full ma glass jist eighteen times. So I play 18 holes—nae mair, nae les…"
>
> There was reason in wha' the ould mon said, an' the cummittee, after appropriate testin' cam' to fuul agreement. An' thas hoo it cam' aboot. Will ye hit furst, while I hae ma' nip?

Personally, I always thought it would be a good idea to have 20 holes. We would still record our score for only 18 of them, which means we could drop our two worst holes before totaling our round. I don't know about you, but it seems that no matter how well I'm playing, there always seems to be two real bad holes that screw up my entire day somewhere during the round.

In fact, the PGA West Course designed by Tom Weiskopf in La Quinta, California, has a 19th hole. For those who like to bet, it's a great way to break a tie; for those who want to trade a bad hole for another chance, it's a great way to change your scorecard.

Here's how we play it: When my friends and I reach the 18th green, we tally our scores. Anyone in the group who has had a fairly good round spoiled by one or two holes can elect to "roll the bones," so to speak. He can play the 19th and replace his worst hole with the score on the 19th. However, if his performance on the 19th turns out to be worse than the hole he wanted to replace, he has to add 6 strokes to his final score and pay each of us $10.

Why the Hole Gets Smaller the Closer You Get to It

In the beginning days of golf, the ball was hit at posts stuck in the ground. The Scots later invented the hole, which is the primary reason Scotland is considered the home of golf.

The hole—so simple, so necessary, so stationary, and yet so hard to find! In fact, the hole is the entire point of the game. No matter how badly you do it, you must get the ball into that little orifice. The actual hole is about 4 inches across and about 6 inches deep.

One of the many contradictions of golf involves the hole: The closer you get to it the smaller it looks. This defies physics, of course, but is nevertheless true. When you are about to tee off, the hole might as well be a 100-foot-wide crater made by an ancient meteor, but as you slowly approach it, one miserable shot at a time, you will find that it actually appears smaller, and when you finally reach the green, it looks like a thimble.

Many players have proven this theory. If you are 60 feet away from the hole on the outer fringes of a green when the pin is still in place, it appears to be a fair-sized cavity. However, if you are about to attempt an 18-inch putt for big bucks, the hole suddenly puckers up to the size of a penny. This is due to two facts. First, in comparison to the diameter of the flag pin stuck in it, the hole appeared as a huge hungry mouth just waiting to gobble up your ball. Second, once everyone's on the green and the pin is removed, it's your turn to perform a miracle in front of your group. Naturally your nerves seize up and the hole shrinks to the size of the period at the end of this sentence.

The entire putting ritual reminds me of a conversation I once had with a psychologist who was talking to me about facing my fears. He said,

> Your fears come mostly from your own internal perception of things, not from actual danger, unless, of course, you have a Mafia hit contract out on you, in which case your fears are real. Here's an example: If I were to place a 20-foot-long piece of 2-by-4 wood on the floor of my office and ask you to walk across it from end to end, you probably wouldn't have any problem getting to the other side without falling. If, on the other hand, I placed that same 20-foot board across the tops of two adjacent 10-story buildings and asked you to walk across it, you would probably have some trepidation. Putting is just like that.

He was a weird guy, but he made sense to me.

In 1996, at the Toshiba Classic held at the Newport Beach Country Club in California, a senior tour professional (who shall remain unidentified by this first-hand reporter—why rub it in?), 4 putted from 18 inches out! That hole must have looked mighty small to him. His first stroke went just right of the hole, rimmed it, and rolled out to the left and down a small hill. Still only 18 inches away, he putted back up and rimmed it to the right, this time sending it about 10 inches out. He then putted past the right of the hole by about a 1/2-inch and finally managed to put the ball in the cup on his fourth try.

It's odd how I was affected by watching that. I felt total empathy for him and I had to catch my breath a little after each failed stroke. But, when he was done, I felt good in a strange way, knowing that even the best golfers blow it sometimes. On the other hand, we amateurs can occasionally hit a great shot or sink a spectacular putt as well as the pros. It's one of the reasons we become addicted. Think about it: just about everyone at some point has hit an unbelievable putt or pitched the ball near the hole from 60 yards out.

What other game could we claim to play as well as the guys who earn millions, even if only for 1 second. Nobody I know could hit a ball over the center field fence at Yankee stadium, throw a perfect spiral to a speeding receiver 65 yards downfield, or shoot a jumper over Jordan. But I have seen some unbelievable putts, pitches, and drives by guys who never even played sports in high school.

Sometimes I think that the longer putts are easier to make than the very short ones. The longest successful putts on record in a major tournament were both 110 feet and were made by Bobby Jones in the 1927 British Open and Nick Price in 1992. Bob Cook sank a 140-footer at St. Andrews in a Pro-Am tournament in 1976.

Personally, I would rather have a putt that's just off the green. In fact, I've made so many more of those putts than the ones on the green that I prefer this lie. It's probably because we're allowed to leave the pin in the hole when putting or chipping from off the green, and more often than not the pin stops the ball and drops it into the hole.

Acing a hole must be an incredible rush. I won't find out until I'm past 70 years old, though. It seems that most of the holes-in-one are achieved, not by professionals or younger players as you might expect, but by skinny old men who look like they couldn't raise a stick let alone hit a hole-in-one.

As an example, the retired husband and wife golf team of Elmer and Marilyn James from Potsdam, New York, recently celebrated beating the odds with a "two-in-one" special. While both were playing in the same foursome at the Halifax Plantation in Ormond Beach, Florida, Elmer shot a hole-in-one on the 181-yard, par-3 16th. Not to be outdone, his wife Marilyn came up next and aced it too! I have read that the odds of an amateur hitting a hole-in-one are around 35,000 to 1; you could figure that one on a dime store calculator. The odds on Elmer and Marilyn's miracle would require the use of a Univac for a week.

The longest regulation hole made in 1 stroke was a shot at the 10th at the appropriately named Miracle Hills Golf Club in Omaha. In 1965, Robert Mitera, all of 5 feet 6 inches tall and weighing in at 165 pounds, drove his ball 245 yards to a drop-off, where it continued in a stiff downhill wind another 195 yards and fell into the cup, a total of 440 yards away! And the greatest number of legitimate holes-in-one achieved by a single person is reported to be Norman Manley of California with 47 to date.

Who Is the Most Powerful Man in Golf?

No, it's not Tiger Woods, Arnold Palmer, or Jack Nicklaus. It's not even Ely Callaway. It's the greenskeeper. Remembering how difficult it is to get that little ball into that tiny hole, think about some of the impossible pin placements you've been faced with.

The greenskeeper is the most powerful man in all of golf because he decides where to dig the hole. Each night he sneaks onto the course with his funny little post-hole digger that extracts a perfect cylinder in one sudden and violent movement in whatever place pleases him—generally, the more inaccessible the better. Have I convinced you yet? He's the most powerful man in golf and we are all at his mercy. He's also the third grumpiest course employee behind the first and second place winners—the starter and the marshal, respectively.

Reading the Greens—Or Successful Plumb-Bobbing

Getting the ball into the hole with the fewest strokes possible always necessitates "reading" the green. Bad golfers will treat this "read" like *War and Peace* rather than the comic strip it is. My rule of thumb is that the worse the golfer is, the longer the novel.

Golfers who dream they will come anywhere near par someday and who want to appear savvy will read the greens with the greatest care, using many techniques. The most popular is "plumb-bobbing." Plumb-bobbing is part showmanship, part surveying, and mostly wasting time. This technique requires that the golfer squat down and hold his putter up between his face and the hole. It is rumored that this will tell the astute observer which way the green is sloping and which way the grass is growing, provided he has plumbed with his dominant eye. I have never figured out which is my dominant eye, so this technique has not been particularly successful for me. As for which way the grass is growing—everyone knows, it's up!

Some greens are more difficult to read than others. Take, for instance, the world's largest green on the 7th hole at the International Golf Club in Boston, Massachusetts, a par-6, 695-yard monster with a green area in excess of 28,000 square feet! Try to read *that* one. Reading it correctly would be like finishing off the *Encyclopedia Britannica* in less than 10 minutes. I could be the mayor of this green, which has more undulations than a python doing a belly dance. This single green is larger than some of the golf courses I've played. (Well, okay, you get the point.) What possible good could it do to read it, other than to impress your fellow golfers with your plumb-bobbing technique?

Another technique is to lay your putter down as straight as possible, carefully placing the head toward the hole and the shaft pointing back to you. I'm not sure what this is supposed to accomplish other than to infuriate the foursome behind you, who know that you don't know what you're doing and that you're not going to make the putt anyway.

Actually, determining which way the grass is growing (besides up) is also helpful. This is known as "the grain." The next time you are watching golf on television, you may notice that before the pros putt they will walk up and look down into the hole intently—if they're playing on Bermuda greens. The reason: they're looking to see which way the grass is growing. Not all grass actually grows up. Some of it, like Bermuda, grows sideways.

Because Bermuda grows sideways, mowing it exposes the roots on one side enough so, as the sun shines on it during the day, the side of the hole that has the root exposed is slightly brownish, whereas the other side of the hole is still green. This tells the veteran player the direction of the grain.

One of My Favorite Holes

Of all the holes I've ever played, one jumps to mind immediately as the most memorable. I treasure this hole—not for its beauty or challenge, but for its entertainment value.

Alongside one of the oceanside holes at a course that shall remain anonymous, next to a Ritz-Carlton Hotel, there lives a young, rich, and beautiful woman. I don't know her name, nor have I ever been formally introduced. My friends and I have never carded a par on this short 3 even though it is a very easy hole. The reason? We are always distracted but not by your normal annoyances like noise, or flying insects, or chattering partners, mind you.

Each time we approach the green, there she appears on the balcony of her majestic estate—stark naked! Luscious, beautiful, alluring, and mischievous, her only accessory is a cigarette in a long black holder, straight from central casting. Because her balcony is made of wrought iron, she is quite visible from head to toe as she gracefully strides back and forth with a demure smile aimed in our direction. As you might imagine, it is quite difficult to concentrate on a putt or much of anything else when presented with such an entertaining show. It's funny how this hole always gets bunched up.

There we are on the green, pretending to line up our putts, forever plumb-bobbing, checking every conceivable angle, each blade of grass, more plumb-bobbing, laying our clubs down, aiming at the hole, surveying and, yet, despite all of our meticulous preparation, I've been known to take up to 8 putts to sink the ball. All the while, as we look back at the fairway, there are at least three groups stacked up behind us, livid with impatience. Of course, they never know what's in store for them until they, too, reach the green. At the next hole we always share big knowing winks and grins as they finally come up behind us.

I don't know how long she stays out there smoking her cigarette and parading about, but I know she must get a big kick out of all the commotion because she's there most every time we've played that hole.

Hole Tips

Now that you've seen, heard, and learned all about the incredible shrinking hole, I'll leave you with some final thoughts:

- It's easier to sink putts from the fringe than the green because you're allowed to use the pin as a backstop. So quit trying so hard to get on the dance floor and just flop it up there on the edges. Even the great Ben Hogan used this technique. In tight match play, depending on the circumstances, he would sometimes lay up on a par 3, knowing he had a good chance to chip in from the edges and, at the very worst, sink the ball in 4.

- Do not think about the hole until you are on the green. For most of your shots you won't be able to see it, so why distract yourself with hole thoughts. You're far better off concentrating on good club selection and course management.

- Think of it this way: There is only one thing in golf that does not move—the hole. It should be quite easy to coax the ball in there. Remember that the hole is home to the ball. This is its true resting place—where it feels most secure. The ball really does want to go home. Like Adam Sandler's uninvited golf guru said in the movie *Happy Gilmore*, "It wants to go home, you just gotta give it a plane ticket."

- Don't be one of those people who sticks his putter down into the hole to retrieve the ball; it ruins the edge of the hole and probably the next player's putt.

- Always putt out, even if your friends give you a "gimmie." If you don't, you're missing one of the sweetest sounds in golf.

— CHAPTER 6 —

SWINGING FOR THE MOON

The swing is *the* thing. For the entire first 2 years of my golf odyssey, I didn't work on anything other than my swing. I never tried to fade the ball, draw, cut, or in any other manner affect its flight other than to hit it as far and as straight as I could. My goal, as they say, was to "groove my swing." In other words, to develop a beautiful, flawlessly fluid motion that mimicked Freddie Couples—a swing that would never leave or fail me. A swing that would begin with a slow, uninterrupted, pendulum-like motion with neither a twitch or stutter, and continue back around and through the ball without a hint of effort.

I would become the Fred Astaire of golfers. Once I had achieved this state of bliss, I would then begin to master the various subtleties of the game including shot shaping, course management, club selection, and low, low scores. Ha! Sure!

It is said that a good and reproducible swing is the result of many, many repetitions that eventually develop muscle memory. Once your muscles can remember the drill, your mind can let go and you can just play without standing over the ball like a statue for 15 minutes, trying to remember *any* combination of the thousands of swing mechanics that are possible. And there are at least thousands, according to Mac O'Grady and his MORAD project. Who is Mac O'Grady and what is MORAD?

Good questions. Mac was once tied for the lead in the U.S. Open. Some years ago he was charging up the back on the final round just 1 or 2 strokes behind Tom Watson, Scott Simpson, and Seve Ballesteros. He came close but didn't win. Mac was known as a really quirky guy who was constantly warring with what he called, the "totalitarian officials." He even punched out a spectator at an event once. He could hit the long ball and lob a hundred of them into a soup can from 100 yards. Mac wasn't all mouth though and was often referred to as the best pure ball-striker in golf—the man with the perfect swing! In fact, he was obsessed with the mechanics of it.

Mac went on to become a golf-swing guru with a flock of devotees known as "Macolytes." Eventually, his obsession with the swing led to a complete life study, which he called MORAD, or the "McCord O'Grady Research and Development" project. Incredibly complex, the CAD computer model he developed features 10 segments or ideal positions, from address to follow-through. These 10 segments, not being enough, were broken down into 10 subsegments, each of which contains the proper position for 13 body parts. Mac's computer analysis then specifies, in three dimensions, 3,900 variables per swing. More of his refinements are contained in reams of charts with every variable optimized for each club including hooks, draws, fades, and slices, and high, low, and medium trajectories.

Talk about a man obsessed, Mac's model contains 187,200 variables and he is intimately acquainted with all of them. The next time you feel like you're mired in six different swing thoughts that completely distract you from playing by instinct, or your mind refuses to let you "play" the game, just be thankful you're not one of Mac's students.

Did You Know Your Muscles Have Brains?

The difference between Mac's approach and the real world is called "muscle memory." I'm told that muscle memory is a biological and chemical fact. Each cell in your body contains its own little brain. Thus all the cells in your arms, shoulders, and torso—the ones used most to swing a golf club—have the capability of remembering. I think mine have Alzheimer's. They've hammered nearly a million balls out onto the driving range and they still can't remember the same swing plane from one week to the next.

One day my swing is effortless, and nearly every shot is pure, sweet contact. My tempo and rhythm are internalized, a ballet in my mind. When this occurs I don't care what my score is. I played like this last week—shot a 93 and felt like I'd scored in the 70s. I didn't care that I hadn't reached my usual 86 or 87. It was a sublime feeling and is one of the major reasons we all continue to hack away, year after year, even when one horrible day of golf follows another. We keep coming back for more, fruitlessly trying to replicate that euphoria.

Every 5 or 6 months, even if I've been playing well—indeed grooved my swing—out of nowhere a flulike disease will afflict me. It comes without warning. It's called "the shanks."

There is absolutely nothing worse that could happen to a golfer. I would not wish this on Attila the Hun. What feels like the perfect swing produces an almost sideways ball flight. If it happens when I'm on the driving range, my ball most invariably strikes the guy standing closest to my right. It's actually almost an impossible shot to make if you're trying to do it, and believe me, I've been in situations where I would've loved to have made the ball travel perpendicular to my body; but it can't be planned.

The moment it happens, I break out in a cold sweat. My heart beat elevates dramatically, and I stop, motionless, as a wave of panic and nausea floods over me. Usually, I'll take a deep breath, back away for a moment, regroup, and hope it was just a freakish one-of-a-kind accident. If my next two swings produce the same effect, I promptly pick up my clubs and walk off the range, knowing there is no hope.

This sad state of affairs has afflicted me four or five times, and I know from experience that it does not go away quickly. No amount of practice or adjustment to my swing will change it. The shanks come like a bad virus for which there is no known cure. It stays in your system for as long as it likes, for me usually about a week or two and then, just as mysteriously as it came, it disappears.

The 140 MPH Lunge

As we've discussed, one of the primary reasons that equipment manufacturers are making millions upon millions is the universal desire among golfers to hit the ball from today into the year 2002. Some veterans will tell you there are more important elements to dwell on, but I disagree. I think every one of us loves the feeling of hitting the ball dead center in the sweet spot and, in essence, not even feeling the club touch the ball.

As you graduate up the length of the clubs from the wedges to the woods, that feeling becomes more and more intense and pleasurable. Yes, it's great to hit a sweet wedge but it's better to hit a pure 4-iron and, of course, the ultimate rush is the most coveted of all shots: the unadulterated, immaculate conception of a great drive. Where did that come from?

I don't need to describe this because all of you know the feeling, but I will anyway. Now that you've played 13 holes you're finally loose. For some unexplained reason, your body is now balanced and at ease. You decide to take out the lumber, lock and load the big gun. Again, for unexplained reasons you have no swing thoughts. Gone are the "okay, take it back slow, don't rush it, head behind the ball, both Vs pointing to my right shoulder, stay down and out, don't lock my right knee" thoughts. Instead, you draw the long one back slowly and smoothly. Your mind is as empty as a beggar's bank account. Your instincts take over and as you come around it's as if the ball isn't even there. Your club head swipes through it like a speeding locomotive through a pile of whipped cream.

You know instinctively, 1 nanosecond after contact, without ever lifting your head, that the ball is taking off in a low but rapidly rising trajectory, gaining speed, altitude, and distance, as if it wants to climb to the heavens and visit the golf gods. When it finally comes to rest, it's a frozen rope laid straight down the middle of the fairway, 250 yards away. Everyone in your foursome, especially you, knows that beautiful sound. None of you even need to look to know what has just been achieved, that oh-so rare, long, straight, perfectly struck drive. Not with a 3-wood or even a 2, but a great big, long, almost-impossible-to-hit-well driver. This shot beats a 60-foot putt any day.

Finding the Right Driver for Under $1,000

It has been written that Tiger Woods's swing speed through contact is about 135 MPH. To put this in perspective, the average weekend player's swing speed is about 80 MPH. Exponentially speaking, the 65 MPH difference in these two speeds is actually closer to 650 MPH. This phenomenal speed is what gives Tiger's balls vigor. His drives, as well as those of several other pros who hit the ball past 300 yards, also contribute to the millions that are made by equipment makers. All of us want to hit the ball as far as the pros, and so we continue to spend more and more money on the "right" driver and the "right" balls. No matter how much our conscious mind knows that it isn't our driver that's the problem, our subconscious mind keeps writing checks.

For years manufacturers have been making club heads, particularly drivers, bigger and bigger and bigger, whereas the old standard Wilson woods, which younger readers will be surprised to know were actually made of wood, were puny compared to today's behemoths. The old drivers were about 135 cubic centimeters (cc), while some of today's titanium heads measure more than 300 cc. They look like a boxing glove stuck on the end of a toothpick. A new competitor debate has just entered the arena though: the shallow-faced woods. These manufacturers claim that big is out, shallow and smaller is in, just as it was 20 years ago. And now some manufacturers are even abandoning our newest best friend—titanium—and going back to steel. That's like going back to the cave men days of golf! What are they thinking?

Every teacher will tell that you the driver is the most difficult club in your bag to hit well. For this reason, the design and manufacturing of drivers is one of the most profitable areas of the golf equipment industry. Any nuance that the marketers can come up with that promises that you will be able to hit a driver longer and straighter will produce phenomenal sales. I know this from first-hand experience. It's embarrassing to admit, but I have owned more than 10 different drivers in the last 30 months. Each one of them cost more than $350. No matter how keenly I'm aware that my driving problem has little to do with the club, I continue to search for the equipment "fix." Thankfully, most retailers took my "old" drivers back in trade each time some new club caught my fancy. But, since most were only a week "old," my losses were substantial. Not only didn't I get much use out of them, but my trade-in value was about 60 percent of the original cost. I estimate that this trading spree has cost me more than $2,000 over the last 2-1/2 years.

How I Tried to Find the World's Best Driver in Anchorage, Alaska

I've been told time and again not to listen to tips from other golfers, whether it's about my swing or a particular club. Everyone swings differently and gets a different reaction out of any given set of clubs. That doesn't matter to me, because I listen to everyone. Two months ago I was at the range and was hitting my driver quite well. Most balls were straight and reaching the 240 mark on the fly. An elderly gentleman next to me, who looked to be about 83, was using a driver I had never seen. Although his rickety body was having trouble raising the club higher than his belt, he nevertheless managed to strike the ball quite well and consistently sent it out about 200 yards. However, as soon as he returned to hitting his irons, his shots were just about as feeble as his body. "Aha!" I thought. "There must be magic in that unusual driver of his."

As he was taking a respite on the bench, I approached him and asked to see his driver. It had a shallow face and was much smaller than mine and had an odd shape. I didn't recognize the manufacturer's name and thought it was custom-made. As I was inquiring about his club, he wholeheartedly encouraged me to try it. My first ball sailed effortlessly out to about 250 yards as did my second, third, and most subsequent shots thereafter. As I returned his magic club, I inquired where he got it. He wheezed his answer back, "My son sent it to me from Anchorage, Alaska, as a Father's Day gift."

I remember back when I was already hitting my newest driver 240 yards on a rope, the one I'd only had for 3 weeks. Even though I was only getting another 10 yards out of this old man's club, I knew I had to have one. Since I didn't recognize the manufacturer, my first thought was to get his son's phone number. Most people would have told me to take a hike, but grandpa was obliging. He wrote his son's work number on a matchbook and gave it to me. Not only was I bold enough to borrow his club, but I had been persistent enough to obtain his son's phone number.

I thanked the stranger and returned home, whereupon I immediately dialed the number in Alaska. Unfortunately, the company did not know who the man was. In my haste I hadn't thought to get the stranger's number, a dead end to be sure—for most people, that is.

I had to have that club. I had to find out who made it and where I could buy one. So out I set to locate the manufacturer and where I could write a check. The Internet proved unsuccessful as did Interpol. The PGA, USGA, and WPGA were no help. More than 50 phone calls to retailers didn't pan out. I asked friends, strangers on the range, wholesalers—all without gaining a clue. I even thought of hiring a private detective. To this day I do not know who makes that club, but I did manage to waste more than 2 weeks of my time trying to find out. Such is the craving for the longer and straighter drive.

Fortunately, I have now found my driving prowess, at least temporarily and I love the Titleist 975 deep-face driver I use. For the first time ever I am able to drive the ball more than 240 yards on the fly, and I owe it all to my new driver—for now.

Finding Your Swing—Again

If you are new to the game, you will need to find and keep a swing that works for you. Even if you're a veteran, from time to time we all lose our swing. Where it goes, no one knows. Somehow, what you thought was ingrained forever is now hopelessly irretrievable, or so it seems.

In my mind, even though golf is a game of strict rules, there are exceptions, especially when it comes to my swing. With that in mind, try to remember the last time you lost yours. Imagine yourself poised at the first tee, where just about all of us get nervous. This is the only hole you will play today where you will have an audience larger than four people. In all likelihood, the gallery will be backed up and you'll have about 100 eyeballs zeroed in on your swing. The USGA rules state that a player who assumes his stance and formally addresses the ball and then fairly strikes at it, but in so doing fails completely to make contact with any part of the ball, is deemed to have taken a stroke, or words to that effect.

If your swing has deserted you and you do indeed whiff and, in the process, displace three disks and reorient four lumbar vertebrae hexagonally to one another as I have, this is what you must do and do immediately:

Do not speak. Do not utter a single syllable. Without hesitation or pause, stay in the batter's box and readdress the ball. Do not exhibit any dismay, surprise, or disgust by facial expression or motion, or offer an other indication that you harbored any notion that you were indeed actually attempting to strike the ball. Make no comment other than a statement to the effect that it was most for-tuitous your practice swing was poor, which, since everything in golf is just the opposite of what you think it is, means, that your now true, intended, final, real, and accountable stroke will most certainly be a beauty!

Three-time British Open champion Henry Cotton, playing in the 1956 U.S. Open at Oak Hill with a putt of less than a foot for bogey, whiffed the ball or made some sort of unthinking movement near it; no one is quite sure which. His competitors swore he did make a full swing. Cotton claimed to have lost his balance, never intending to take a stroke. The USGA was in a dilemma: Did he or didn't he? They finally sided with Cotton, citing a lack of substantial contrary proof. He got away with it.

If your swing continues to desert you into a round and should you ever strike the ball atrociously by sculling, slicing, or in any other manner sending your ball poorly on its journey, and if you have the great good fortune to find it has hit a tree, bounced off a rock, or skipped over a lake onto the green or in any other desirable destination, make no declaration of surprise either through facial expression or verbal astonishment. If you get a lucky bounce and everyone has witnessed it, you will be told so by each in your foursome. However, you should still remain silent and not divulge the true nature of your swing. Instead try to remember all of those shots in the past that you thought were going to be perfect yet wound up behind a tree 8 feet in diameter. You deserve the good luck the golf gods have just bestowed on you. When you skull, yank, pull, or otherwise strike the ball poorly and it still finds a great lie, your silence will have the effect of removing the question of luck from the minds of your fellow golfers. They will not have any alternative but to congratulate you. For, as all golfers know, the game is steeped in etiquette, and since there was a 50/50 chance that you did hit the ball well, they will have to go with that polite assumption.

Revisiting Swing Thoughts

Why is it that when you go to the range to practice the day following a lesson or even the day after you hit 200 balls well, all the swing thoughts or keys you could have sworn you had memorized and ingrained mysteriously evaporate from your brain? I never can seem to remember a single one of the keys until I've hit so many balls that once the keys *do* start to come back to me, I'm too tired to hit any more.

Yet when I go out to play and I'm *not* supposed to bring any swing thoughts with me and I'm told to just let my muscle instincts take over, I remember every single key on each and every shot. No matter how hard I try not to think of these keys, as I approach tee shots my mind races through hundreds of potential swing thoughts.

Here's a sampling of what goes through my mind from the time I address the ball until the time I actually make contact—a period of less than 3 seconds:

> Keep my head behind the ball. Am I balanced? Remember, low and slow. Take the club away with your arms, shoulders, and torso as one piece. Don't break down your wrists. Make a full shoulder turn. Did I forget to turn off the stove at home? See the club head hit the ball. Don't look up. Keep your right knee flexed. Don't let your left knee bend out, bring it in to the right as you make your turn. Visualize the ball on a string and see the flight and landing spot. Make sure the club head is outside your hands at all times. Let your wrists hinge naturally. Hit down and out. Throw your hands down the target line and oh, one last thing—remember to follow through.

When you learn to let go of control and make your mind a vast wasteland devoid of any thoughts, only then will you be able to strike the ball well when playing.

Is a Putt a Swing?

According to the golf gods, we are only allowed 14 clubs in our bag, including the putter. Personally, I don't feel the putter should be considered a club, just as the manipulation of it should not be considered a swing. Think about how much lower our scores would be if we didn't have to count our putts as swings, nor our putters as clubs. This way we could eliminate at least 40 strokes from our scores and carry yet another wedge. We'd all be shooting 82s. If as we must, count our putts as swings, this is the perfect place to analyze the stroke's unfortunate necessity within the game and to lobby for its removal when calculating our scores.

The putt is the antithesis of all other swings. All professionals and teachers will tell you there is only one swing for all clubs, be it a 5-foot-long driver or a 7-iron. You and I know this is patently impossible. The swing path of my driver comes from an entirely different angle and speed than any of my other clubs. When my 7-iron is at the top of my backswing, still arching up, the head of my driver would already have whistled past the tee, hopefully taking the ball with it, and continued all the way around and fully through my follow-through, and as I stood there posing nicely would have hit me in the ass.

How can we seriously say that a putter is a club and its manipulation a swing if it's true that we are supposed to use the same swing for all clubs. Even the great Ben Hogan said of the putt, "There is no similarity between golf and putting. They are two different games. One is played in the air and the other on the ground." Add to this Sam Snead's comment, "I shot a wild elephant in Africa 30 yards from me, and it didn't hit the ground until it was at my feet. I wasn't a bit scared, but a 4-foot putt scares me to death."

Mac O'Grady has already proven through computer analysis that there are more than 187,200 different mechanical aspects and movements when you swing your woods and irons. Thank the golf gods we're only cognizant of about a hundred of them. We refer to them as swing keys, which we've already discussed. Comparatively, the simple pendulum-like stroke of a putt, which uses only the arms and shoulders, taking the putter head less than 18 inches, front to back, should not be considered a swing. It is, however, and I will tell you why. The same computer analysis that discovered 187,200 mechanics in the swing of the other "true" clubs has found only two in the putt: back and forth. No ups, no downs, no arounds or anything else. For some unknown reason golfers find this an impossible notion. There must be more to it, otherwise why would it be so difficult to get the ball into the hole from such short distances and on such nice surfaces? So we assign almost as many swing keys to the putt as the drive, to whit:

> Head down. Hear the ball fall in the cup, don't see it.
> Is this an uphill lie? Which way is the grain going? Is
> this green fast or slow? I wonder if that chick I met
> last night will return my call. Align my body perpen-
> dicular to the hole. Grip lightly and remember to use
> only your arms and shoulder. No lower body or wristy
> movements. On and on it goes. Do I take the putter
> back farther if this is a longer putt, or do I take it back
> about the same as a short putt, but follow through far-
> ther? Is this the right putter in the first place, or
> should I go back to that one with the short handle I
> have in the garage with my 16 other old putters?

All these questions and anxieties for a stroke that is essentially a simple back-and-forth level movement of less than 18 inches, all on a very smooth, generally well-kept surface. Compare the complexity of this simple, unadorned, straight-forward movement with that of hitting a full iron or 3-wood out of the secondary, or even in the fairway. To sum up: Craig Stadler at the 1993 U.S. Open said, "Why am I using a new putter? Because the old one didn't float too well."

Swing Tips

You'll probably spend all of your golf life trying to find and perfect your swing. The following tips certainly couldn't hurt—and might even help:

- The only place you should practice your swing is on the range or in your garage in front of a mirror. When you're ready to play, just lock, load, and shoot.
- Empty your mind of all thoughts before you start to play. This is not easy, but there is a technique that will help you learn to do it. Just sit in a chair for 15 minutes and try not to think about a red elephant. At first, your mind will race through a thousand thoughts while trying not to think about the elephant, but after a few minutes your mind will become a blank slate. After you become proficient at this technique, you can use it on the course, when too many swing thoughts start to come to mind. You can also try counting sheep.
- When you're practicing in the garage in front of a mirror, use an old, worn-out tire to hit with an old club. Place the tire so that the back edge is about where your ball would be, then practice hitting it. What this does for your swing is to teach you where and what impact is. Because our swings are continuous movements, or at least should be, we're not visually aware of where our hands, arms, and body are when the club head is making contact with the ball. Hitting the tire in front of the mirror will give you a great visual idea of what impact looks like.

CHAPTER 7

WHY ALL STARTERS ARE GRUMPY

There is only one starter in the entire world with a smile on his face—and he's dead. All the starters that are still with us are very unhappy, at least those who work at public courses. Why? First of all, starters have to get up *way* too early. They have to get to the course even before the real addicts arrive at sunrise. Second, they don't get to play much; they have to stand around all day and watch everyone else have fun.

What Exactly Do Starters Do?

Mostly, they boss everyone around, act extremely aloof, and provide witty retorts to your questions. But besides that, they get all the players out onto the course in a timely manner, which generally means a pace of about 10 minutes between groups. I've found that this window has now narrowed to about 7 minutes on many courses because of the growing appeal of the game. And where there used to be occasional "twosomes" and "threesomes," now there are only "foursomes" and "fivesomes." Pretty soon there will be only "sevensomes."

The starter's job is a little like being an air-traffic controller at a major airport. Just as the controller must keep planes separated by time and distance, the starter must try, with the help of the marshal, to keep just the right distance—which they think is about 225 yards—between groups. Remember, if you're not keeping up with the group in front of you, you're holding up the group behind you. It's a giant daisy chain.

All this rush is about two things: First, making money. Second making the game enjoyable for as many people as possible. It's not fun to play slowly, but neither is it fun to be pushed to race through the day, especially by an overzealous marshal.

Let's do some calculating. Assume, for example, a southern California public golf course charges $125 a round, including a cart. Play begins at sunrise; in the summer that's about 5:45 A.M. If you figure an average of one foursome every 10 minutes, and that the starter has groups starting until 4:30 P.M, a club can fit about 65 groups into a summer day; that's $32,000 per day. Of course in the winter this number drops because the days are shorter; so let's suppose revenues are roughly 65 percent of the summer "take" per day; that's $21,000, give or take a few dollars.

Further, considering cheaper rates at twilight and during the week, I figure this amounts to a year-round average of about $25,000 per day, 7 days a week. That's nearly $10 million a year.

Starting Pay for a Starter

Although more than $12 billion is spent annually on green fees and carts, the starter doesn't get much of this. In fact, starting pay for a starter must be minimum wage. All day long he hauls in buckets of cash or credit card receipts and listens to the cash register ring with the sound of money. At day's end, the tally is nearly $30,000 in revenues. His cut? Forty-four dollars, before taxes!

As each new group comes into the shop, the starter watches as they tote their $2,000 sets of clubs and prance around in their $125 Izod golf shirts. And between the groups who have reserved starting times, there are always dozens of "drop bys" who don't have a reservation but want to squeeze onto the waiting list, which is already four pages long. At regular intervals during the day, they will come back to harangue the starter, angry that they haven't been called to play yet. They're like kids in a back of the station wagon, setting out on a long vacation. Before the car's gone 2 miles they chant, "Are we there yet? Are we there yet?"

Let's recap: A starter rises at 4 A.M. His first customers are unhappy about something and tell him so. He doesn't get to play. He has to watch everyone else have fun all day in expensive clothes using really nice equipment. And, finally, he really wants to be on the pro tour but knows he doesn't have the talent. That's why the starter is always grumpy. Having said all this, I'll probably have to start making reservations under an assumed name.

Getting a Starting Time before Midnight

At the more popular courses—which is just about all of them, if you want a specific starting time for your twosome or foursome—you must make reservations just as you would in a popular restaurant.

Unfortunately, as poor as starters are, they cannot be bribed. Offering a starter a $20 bill, as you might do with the maître d' at a Las Vegas dinner show, will not get you a better start time, nor will it make him smile. If nothing else, starters pride themselves in their power to organize a good long orderly line. Unlike a maître d', who can make thousands of dollars in tips, the starter doesn't understand that he could augment his feeble salary with tips from those more, shall we say, "dedicated" customers.

Making reservations for a specific starting time is a weekly year-in, year-out ritual. Most courses will take reservations only 7 days prior to play. You can make reservations in advance of 7 days if you're a tourist coming to town and want to ensure a tee time, but it will cost you extra. Not only will you pay $150 to play, but you will pay another $25 surcharge for having the good sense to call early. This is not considered good planning—it's called a "privilege."

Imagine with me now as we dial up Alfredo's Restaurant, known for its particularly good chicken primavera, for a reservation in 2 weeks and are told that a $25 fee will be added to our bill for the privilege of making a reservation in advance of 7 days!

Well, that just goes to show how addictive the game is! Because we all want to play so desperately, we feign respect for the starter and try not to anger him too much.

With a 7-day window, most popular courses won't begin taking reservations for next weekend until this Saturday beginning at 6:00 A.M. Of course, what you don't know if you haven't played for long or aren't a member of that club is that members automatically get preferential starting times, meaning anything before noon. This leaves precious few spots open, even if you—by some miracle bestowed on you by the golf gods—are the very first one to get an open phone line to the starter at precisely 6 A.M. I've experimented with this policy by actually setting my alarm clock (on an otherwise beautiful Saturday, when I wouldn't have gotten out of bed before 9 A.M. under any other circumstances) to the god-awful hour of 5:30 A.M. To try to get a jump on the 6:00 A.M. call-in time, I dialed my test starter at 5:45 A.M. Guess what? The line was already busy and it wasn't even 6 A.M. yet. And the line stayed busy for an hour, even though I used my special 500 megahertz, computer-driven, auto phone redialer, which can dial any 10-digit number in less than 1/2 second more than a thousand times in succession. When I finally got through and asked the starter what his first available time was for next Saturday, he snarled, "First time's at 4:38 P.M." I questioned, "How can a complete round of 18 holes be finished before nightfall?" His answer? "Play fast."

Once when I was able to reach the starter at 6:10 A.M., the best time he could give me was 2:25 P.M. When I protested, the starter told me, "Take it or leave it. I got a lotta lines going, gotta go." Of course my answer was, "I'll take it, I'll take it!" Thank God I got a time. I had already promised my best client we'd play at this course this weekend. Of course, I didn't tell him he'd have to bring his flashlight.

Tips on Dealing with the Maître d'

There is no perfect way to handle the starter, but here are some suggestions on ways to work with him:

- Never smile at a starter. He hates this and you'll automatically go to the bottom of the list. If you mirror his frown he will empathize with you and think you're as unhappy as he is. (And, after all, it isn't that difficult to frown: remember, you're going to play golf!)
- Do not back sass the starter or you may find yourself sitting on a concrete bench, in the blazing sun, for the better part of the day, mistakenly thinking you are going to play golf.
- Put your name on the wait list, and when the starter snarls, "Might not be able to get you out for 3 or 4 hours, we're having a tournament," just say, "Yes sir. I'll just be sitting here on the bench until I hear my name called. Did you get the spelling of my name right? That's Robert—R, O, B, E, R, T!"
- Do not try to bribe the starter. This is not technically a jailable offense, but it is considered gauche.

— CHAPTER 8 —

ZEN AND THE ART OF NOT SCORING

The most elusive aspect of the game of golf is par. Getting the ball in the hole is the first objective, no matter how many strokes it takes. Manners and good etiquette are also meaningful, but nothing is more important than par.

What is par? It is the number of strokes that the golf gods have determined to be much less than what you will need to get your ball in the hole. It is assumed that par, which is 72 strokes on most courses, is the number of strokes that it will take a good amateur player or an average professional player to get around the course, putts included. Par gives us the illusion of an attainable goal when, in fact, reaching par is mathematically impossible. This is proven by the fact that out of the 50 million golfers in the world today, only .5 percent shoot par golf. The other 99.5 percent have an average handicap of 25!

In 1959, Sam Snead shot 122 for the lowest-ever score for 36 holes. On the flip side, in 1888, a gentleman named Chevalier Von Cittern finished 18 holes with a total score of 316. That's 17.55 strokes per hole. The .55 probably accounts for all the lip outs. The next worst score over par belongs to Steven Ward who, in 1976, used 222 strokes for the 6,210-yard Pecos Course in Reeves County, Texas, but then Steven was only 3-1/2 years old! That's an average of only 12 shots per hole (he probably even had a few snowmen).

Sometimes scoring becomes downright hideous, even among the pros. A professional golfer on the women's tour once took 166 strokes for a 130-yard, par-3 in Pennsylvania. You read that correctly— 166 strokes on one short hole in a tournament! Her tee shot went into the Binniekil River and the ball floated downstream (she was still using the feathery ball, which floated in water); she got into a boat and rowed after it, eventually beaching her ball 1-1/2 miles away. Although we would call that a true "blow-up" hole, she went on to record a final score of 234. Not bad, if you don't count that one hole and only slightly worse than little Steven's 222.

On each hole, whether it's a par 3, 4, or 5, it is assumed that, if you're a good player, you will take just 2 putts. That means you'll use at least 36 strokes (2 putts times 18 holes) in putting alone. As it's likely you'll have a few 3 putts, the tally will be closer to 39 or 40. That leaves us only a paltry 32 strokes for the entire rest of the course, including tee shots, moon balls, and whacks out of sand, water, trees, elephant grass, ditches, and other obstructions. And this assumes you stay inbounds the entire round without adding in any penalty strokes. Now do you understand why the game is so difficult?

Here is the logic the golf gods used in determining par. On a hole that is up to 250 yards long, they assume scratch players will hit the green with 1 shot and then 2 putts. Any hole that measures up to about 471 yards, it was determined, should be a par 4—the good players are expected to reach the green in 2 shots and then 2 putts. A par 5 is anything beyond 475 yards, and there are some monsters. This does not include the U.S. Open, which routinely changes 490-yard par 5s into 4s for this esteemed once-a-year occasion. They do this to make the pros sweat it for at least one weekend out of the year.

To my knowledge there are no par 2s, and there aren't many holes over par 5. However, there is a hole at the Sano Course at the Satsuki Golf Club in Japan that measures 909 yards! It's a par 7, as well it should be. For me, the yardage in this one hole would equal my score for half the round.

If your total number of strokes matches par, then you have attained a truly enviable state of grace. This is not to say that each hole's par must be matched. You may be fortunate enough to get a birdie—1 stroke under par—once in a while, which would allow you a bogey—1 stroke over par—on some other hole in order to balance the books. This is the only reason the golf gods didn't make every hole a par 5—par 5s are relatively easy and most of the 4s under 410 yards are doable. It's those pesky little par 3s that kill us.

If you are blessed with luck and a certain amount of skill, you may, at some point in your golf experience, shoot an albatross—most people refer to it as a "double eagle" or 3 under par. This is indeed a very pleasant experience, one to be savored the rest of your life. Of course, it would have to occur on a par 5, which generally means about a 520-yard hole. Think about it. Even if your tee shot was 280 yards long, you would still have to hole out on your second shot from 245 yards away! Some folks think it's even more difficult than a hole-in-one.

Let's Just Throw the Ball around the Course and See What Happens

You would think it would be much easier to just throw the ball around the course. You wouldn't have as much distance, but that would be offset by the greater accuracy you would get by throwing the ball as opposed to whacking it with a long stick. What would you guess is the lowest recorded score for throwing a golf ball around a regulation 18-hole course, which is more than 6,000 yards? It's 82! Ladies and gentlemen, that is 10 over par.

If you ever played little league or softball with any success, you know that throwing a ball at a hole should be far easier than trying to hit it into a hole with a foreign object, since the latter just puts one more obstacle between your body and the ball. I guess that logic doesn't apply to golf.

How Not to Score on the Golf Course

As opposed to most sports and games, scoring is easy in golf—it's not scoring that's the challenge. Think about how hard it is for other athletes: Basketball players must constantly put the ball in the hoop; baseball players have to get hit after hit so their team can score. Golfers have none of that silly pressure. All you have to do is hit the ball and you've scored; a note of it is made on your card and in the memories of the three other golfers you're playing with. Your stress comes from trying not to score!

Think of it this way: When you get on the course, you don't want to hit the ball very often. The last thing you want to do is score. So what are you to do?

There are several ways to keep your score low:

- Hit the ball farther on the first two shots.
- Use prayer and body language more often.
- Use pencils with erasers on them.
- Don't take a scorecard with you when you play.

Not keeping score is a great way to reduce stress and allows you to concentrate more on each of your shots. I've done this on several occasions and it helped me to relax and have more fun. If you're not keeping score, a few really bad shots won't ruin the rest of your round.

Remember, golf is a mind game, not a body sport. The art of not scoring is all between your ears, not between your arms. What counts in golf is strategy, course management, and confidence. Look around you. Why do you think all those fat guys with guts hanging over their Sansabelt slacks are shooting in the 70s and your score is in the 90s? It's probably because they've been playing for 40 years, but it also just might have a little to do with their knowledge of the game and their frame of mind.

You must also take into account that you aren't the only one with a mind. We've already discussed that the ball has a brain of its own. I've found that I can coax the ball to do things my way on occasion. Unlike most people, if I hit a big banana slice, I won't lean to the left trying to use body language to magnetically pull the ball back. Instead, I lean in the *same* direction that the ball is traveling. This is called "reverse body language." As I'm leaning I also cajole, "Yeah, baby, go, go, yeah, baby, peel!" I find this annoys the ball, which thought it was going to make me angry by going out-of-bounds; so in retaliation, it will suddenly straighten out and land almost in the fairway. These good results could also be due to the slice-proof new clubs I have, but I like to play it safe. The same body-language technique applies to water. If it's wet on the left, I'll fool the ball by turning my body that way at address and actually aim at the water. Since I know the ball doesn't want to do what I tell it, by aiming at the water I can convince it, most of the time, to find dry land.

Remember, you're not playing against yourself, your cronies, or even the course; you're playing against the ball. When you get ready to make that long putt, use some reverse psychology on it. Tell the ball, "You're not going in that hole. I know you want to go, but I'm not going to let you. I'll tantalize you by letting you kiss its lip but I won't let you rest in your nest." Sure enough that little sphere will race into the hole like a horse heading back to the stables for dinner.

Another important note about the mind game is this: Everything in golf is the opposite of what you think it is. If you're hitting the ball well on the practice range prior to a round, you will inevitably play like you never picked up a stick in your life. The opposite is also quite true. So when you're warming up and hitting the ball badly, don't despair, smile—you're going to have a great day!

Water Ball

On one outing, three of us were playing the Tustin Ranch Golf Course in California. The stranger who was matched with our three-some seemed a quiet, amiable type, but as the day progressed he seemed to be finding the water on all the par 3s and was becoming very frustrated.

Finally, as we reached the 18th hole, a par 4 with a difficult green elevated above a lake, our friend came completely unraveled. His first tee shot fell just inches short of the green and into the water. He promptly took out another ball and tried again. Just as the first one had, his second shot found a watery grave. We knew his anger would preclude him from ever reaching the green so we suggested he just drop on the other side. He retorted, "I'm going to keep hitting this ball until I get one on the green." Nine balls later he gave up, grabbed his bag off the cart, ran to the water's edge, and with a mighty heave threw the entire bag into the pond. By this time we had all finished our putts and were about to go to the clubhouse. Our friend came storming by us and stomped out to the parking lot in disgust. About 10 minutes later, as the three of us were tallying our scores on the patio, our friend came stomping back again. Trying to guess what he was up to, we watched attentively as he marched back down to the pond, sat at the edge, pulled off his shoes, rolled up his pant legs, and waded out into the water.

Once he reached waist depth, he took a deep breath and dove underwater. After a few seconds he lunged back to the surface with his bag, minus a few clubs. It turned out he had left his car keys in his bag. I'm sure he wasn't the first golfer to do the very same thing, but I always wondered why he bothered to roll up his pant legs.

Golf is an extremely subtle game. In the beginning, not scoring is less important than not hitting the ball with the club. After we groove a swing that works and is repeatable, usually within 10 years or so, we must contend with the more delicate, refined, and nearly immeasurable reasons that a swing can come undone. Another truism of golf is that the better your swing gets, the less it takes to set it out of whack. As an example, I can now smash the ball with my driver straight and true like a rope, 245 yards on the fly and, if I'm lucky and the fairway is dry and short, get another 20 yards of roll. As I'm playing a good round and enjoying one fine drive after another, stupidly thinking my good fortune is going to continue throughout the entire round, all of a sudden my swing disappears on the 6th hole, and I'm snap hooking each drive. I feel as if I've been left holding the tab as my gorgeous date hightails it out the back door into a waiting cab with some other guy! Was it my breath? Food in my teeth? Boring conversation? What little subtle thing did I miss?

Invariably, the next day I'll be at the range for hours, fruitlessly trying to figure out what momentous and horrible change my swing plane took or what spasmodic motions my arms are making to cause the problem. It's only when my teacher walks by and casually says, "Robert, you're standing too close to the ball," that the solution is clear. The insignificant positioning of the ball, just 1/64 inch farther forward in my stance, caused all this?

The pros are always on a razor's edge between glory and disaster, and they represent the very limited ranks of fewer than 100 human beings who can make a living at this game, so take heart and listen:

- Tommy Armour once hooked 10 balls out-of-bounds on the 17th hole during the 1927 Shawnee Open, finally carding a 23—the highest one-hole score by any pro in a PGA Tour event. And he had just won the U.S. Open the week before! As good as he was, he could not master the art of not scoring that day.
- Seve Ballesteros, at the naive age of 17, said before the 1974 Spanish Open, "It is impossible for a pro to score in double figures on a hole." He promptly hooked his first drive out-of-bounds, sliced his second out-of-bounds, found water with his sixth, and found the beach with his eighth. He finally putted in for an 11.

Tips to Keep You from Scoring

Although there's no formula to becoming a scratch golfer, here are some tips that might help keep your score down:

- The absolute best piece of advice I ever received in the beginning stages of my golf journey was, "Don't be humble. Get some attitude, no matter how atrociously you play." No matter how badly you play, keep in mind that your friends are at least the lucky recipients of your good company. And as far as the pros being so much better than you, if it weren't for your interest in the game and the consequent television ratings, they'd be playing with you on your municipal course.

- When you are about to play a round, go to the practice range first to find out what swing or stroke you brought that day because every day is different. Once you've determined what your daily special is—be it hook, slice, or an inability to hit the ball entirely—take that swing to the course, because it isn't going to change for the next 5 hours. If you're hooking, just compensate by turning your body more to the right. If you can't even hit the ball, make sure you tell everyone at the first tee that you just had casts taken off both your arms after being run over by a golf cart driven by an angry opponent who lost a lot of money to you.

- Instead of swearing and stomping about, take a deep breath and watch your partner's next shot. In all likelihood it will be just as horrible as yours, and the thought that you're not alone will help to decrease your tension.

- Understand your limitations. If you know in your heart of hearts that you can't hit a 6-iron 170 yards, why try? Forget what the others in your foursome are hitting from the same distance, put your ego aside, and pull out your driver if you have to. After the round is over, no one is going to remember the specific clubs you used and compare them to their own choices. They're just going to remember how bad you were overall.

- If you can putt the ball, do it. The putter is the safest club in golf, although it isn't particularly useful on the greens. There is no rule that says you can't use the putter to hit a nice lie from 150 yards out.

- Bet only when you can afford to lose or when you learn how to cheat better.
- Take some lessons.
- Do not give lessons to your girlfriend or spouse. This is guaranteed to louse up her game on the course and your life when you get home.
- Always use a tee at the tee box on those par 3s. Don't try to play like a pro. The game is much more fun when the ball is in the air.
- Learn to play out of the sand. Learn to love the sand. It's actually easier, in many cases, to get close to the hole hitting out of sand than it is to pull off a difficult chip or a hack out of the rough.
- It is very important to get to the course with plenty of time to warm up and find out whether you brought your slice or your hook with you that day. It is also important to limber up your muscles for the grueling physical activity you are about to undertake. You should arrive at least 2 hours in advance. If your tee time is very early, go to the course the night before and sleep in your car.
- Use pencils with erasers.
- Play a couple of rounds without a scorecard.

CHAPTER 9

HOW TO GET A PASSING GRADE IN CHARM SCHOOL

Only on the golf course—and absolutely nowhere else in civilized society—can you find grown men who are total strangers being quite so polite to each other. Maybe if heads of state conducted themselves as if they were playing golf, there wouldn't be any wars.

No other game employs as much ritual and protocol. That's because there are no referees or umpires, just you and your fellow golfers. Right now, on thousands of courses all over the world, men are hitting big, god-awful-ugly banana slices off the tee and into the next fairway with their $600 drivers, while someone in their foursome is saying, "That'll work." What irks me is when I hit what I think is a good drive and someone still says, "That'll work." You're damn right it will!

No one ever says anything derogatory to a fellow golfer, especially strangers. For all you know, the stranger in your foursome could be the same guy you cut off on the freeway this morning. He yelled obscenities and made finger gestures while you, in turn, retorted with your best verbal assault. But when you get out on the course and realize the same guy is in your foursome, I guarantee you that, at some point during the day, you will still find yourself compelled to massage his ego with a complete lie about his awful shot.

This "praising-of-every-effort" is an integral part of the unwritten table manners of golf. There is a simple reason for this. No one wants anyone else to say anything bad about his swing, so we hedge against this by praising all efforts, no matter how dismal they really are. No matter what goes awry, and mostly everything in golf does, someone in your foursome will find some good in it somehow.

Suppose you make an awful snap hook off the tee into the woods. Your second shot, in an effort to recover, is badly topped and never rises higher than 2 inches off the ground but still manages to roll 75 yards farther than you ever deserved and ends up close to the green. You have just made two of the ugliest shots in golf but someone in your foursome will say, "They don't have pictures on your scorecard, just numbers."

Things you can say when your partner is playing poorly:

- "Hey, we're not playing for *that* much money."
- "I have trouble with that shot too."
- "We should've warmed up longer."
- "I don't play well on the weekends either."
- "Boy, it's a beautiful day isn't it?"
- "That's the only *really* bad shot you've had all day."
- "Where did you get that shirt?"
- "You always play better on the back nine."

And let's not forget the most frequently uttered phrase on the course: "We still have a lot of golf to play." Some guys will still be telling you this right up to the 17th tee.

Unlike the rules of golf, which are well documented, etiquette and manners are just understood, passed down through generations of golfers. There is no USGA etiquette book. Nowhere is this more evident than on the greens, where all players are on their very best behavior.

The Ritual on the Green

Once everyone has reached the green, a unique ritual takes place. This is the area on the course where golfers are the most polite to each other. Not stepping in a fellow golfer's line on the green is a time-honored custom whose practice nears religion. The line is a nebulous area on the green that cuts a direct path between the position of anyone's ball and the hole. It is commonly assumed this path is a swath approximately 6 to 12 inches wide and extends from directly in front of a ball to the hole. Although the ball seldom travels this path, it is politically incorrect to step into it with your spiked shoes. I have never quite figured out the logic behind this ritual because previous golfers have left thousands of spike marks all over the green just prior to your arrival. If five of you are playing, there are so many lines to keep track of that when you need to mark your ball, you have to practically do a cartwheel and a piroutte to avoid them.

Imagine we are all standing and waiting for whoever is "away" (the unfortunate golfer whose ball is farthest from the hole) to putt. We allow him to go first not only because it's proper etiquette but also because we want to see his pain before we go through our own. And it doesn't hurt to see which way his ball wobbles on its doomed-before-it-started journey to the hole either. When the first to putt does miss, there is always a well-mannered, ready-made explanation, "Boy you had the right line." Even though the ball was going 80 miles an hour and never had a chance in hell of going in the hole, I can promise someone will say, "You had the line. You got robbed."

Fore!

Warning your fellow players of impending doom is another time-honored tradition and is always good manners. There is one four-letter word that is used more than any other on the course. No, it isn't *that* word, it's "fore." Contrary to popular opinion, this word did not derive from "forewarned." It came from the shorter "forehead." There is good reason for this. Most of the shots that actually hit someone, hit the person on the forehead. There doesn't seem to be any scientific rationale for this other than Murphy's Law. In all the times I've been on the golf course, I've observed only two unfortunate golfers get hit by a ball. Both were hit dead center on the front of their noggins. The same holds true of all the golf I've watched on television. It's usually a spectator who gets hit and, again, it's always on the head. I have never seen anyone hit on the knee, elbow, or foot, although I'm certain this has been the case somewhere.

Unfortunately, this early warning system of yelling "fore," although good manners, isn't fail-safe. The word "fore" is screamed so often during the day that most players have become deaf to it, with the possible exception of those poor souls who have actually been hit by a ball. With them, any hint of an air-raid warning will bring them to an immediate fetal position behind the nearest solid structure such as a cart, tree, or partner.

The Obligatory 1st Tee and 18th Green Handshake

Another time-honored ritual is the obligatory, first-tee, "How-do-you-do, I'm Robert" handshake, and the "Ralph, (or "gentlemen," if you've forgotten everyone's name), it's-been-a-pleasure-playing-with-you-have-a-nice-day" handshake. I've never, ever played a round of golf without having gone through this well-intended ceremony.

It's interesting to note that on the first tee, the "how-do-you-do" grip is always firm, direct, and manly, but the "it's-been-a-pleasure-adios" clasp as you leave the 18th green depends on how you and your partners played. If you all played well, then the good-bye shake is a sincere "we-shared-a-good-experience" joining of the palms. On the other hand, if you had an abysmal day, your flesh might not actually touch all three of the other guys' palms with such gusto—if at all. The clearly spoken pleasantries you started with now become garbled mumbles of, "Yea, yea, yea; nice playin' with ya." If you all played like crap, and especially if the last hole was the coup de grace of the round, you might end up just scattering like leaves in the wind, thankful the others won't remember your name.

Golf Rage

At some point in time, in the not-so-distant history of golf, rage came out of the locker room and onto the tee boxes and greens. Up until that time, golfers, being gentlemen, would suck in a lot of air, scrunch their eyebrows a little, breathe faster, and keep it all inside, trying to maintain the decorum that is so much a part of good golf etiquette.

Until golf rage became a more visible and oft-demonstrated man-ifestation of the golfer's state of mind, most even-tempered golfers consoled themselves with the thought that those few who dared to stomp around, throw clubs, get into fights, and shout obscenities must be social inferiors who never learned their manners. This is no longer always true.

Although golf appears, on the surface, to be a genteel and extremely polite sport, it can actually be quite violent. These days good manners don't prevent violence but help ensure it is kept to a minimum, with only an occasional club-flinging or breaking.

A few months ago, I was playing at Aviara Golf Course in Carlsbad, California, a very upscale course woven through a community near a Four Seasons Hotel. There are more than a few stately homes along the fairways and greens. On the 16th green my playing partner was about to culminate a "blow-up" hole. He was fuming and spewing forth every obscenity he could think of, using all the seven words comedian George Carlin used to say couldn't be spoken on televi-sion, and then some. A homeowner and his wife were watching and listening from their pool deck near the green. The husband shouted out to my friend, "Hey, keep your language down, there is a woman over here." In response my friend yelled back, "If you didn't want her to hear four-letter words, you shouldn't have moved next to a golf course!"

Terrible things happen when we get golf rage. Ben Crenshaw had to finish the 1987 Ryder Cup putting with his 1-iron after break-ing his putter in a fit of anger. Curtis Strange buried his putter in the ground nearly up to the grip after a particularly bad stroke and was fined $1,000. The legendary Tommy Bolt, known as much for his anger as his play, once said, "If you're going to throw a club, it's impor-tant to throw it ahead of you, down the fairway, so you don't waste energy going back to pick it up." The USGA rule against throwing a club was invented because of Tommy. Upon finding out about the rule at a tournament, he promptly threw his putter in the air and said, "If they're going to fine someone for throwing a club, I'm going to be the first."

Several months ago, while playing on a local municipal course, I was added to a threesome of what appeared to be even-tempered, fairly good-humored golfers. One of them, though, seemed a little higher strung than the other two. Most of his day was devoted to trying to drive his tee shot 500 yards with his new $600 gargantuan titanium driver. Although he was unequivocally the longest driver of the foursome, his accuracy was questionable. As the day wore on, he became more erratic. On the 17th hole he crushed a drive that appeared truly awesome until it reached the 220-yard mark, at which point it took a hard right turn to the east. His grin turned into an upside-down smiley face, as we watched his ball dribble to a halt two fairways over from ours. That was it. He could no longer contain his anger. All decorum vanished. His fuse had reached the flash point. He took his brand new driver and launched it like an Olympic javelin thrower. Its flight was magnificent; in fact, it flew farther than most of my drives that day. After all, those expensive drivers are weighted and balanced perfectly. Whirring like a helicopter blade, it flew over a fence guarding a palatial estate and came to rest—hanging from its giant titanium head— between the slats of the patio cover.

There was total silence on the tee. We all knew better than to make a single comment at that point. Not only was it good manners, but it would help ward off a knuckle sandwich. He paced. He stewed. He swore. And then he stomped off to retrieve his driver.

As he approached the fence, we all caught a glimpse of a man standing in the dining room peering back out at him through the curtains. Our friend yelled to the man, "Sir, would you please come out and give me my very expensive, great Big Bertha™?" The homeowner never budged, never blinked an eye. Apparently, as far as he was concerned, possession was nine-tenths of the law. Our friend yelled out again, this time with more gusto. "Sir, could you please hand me my prized Big Bertha™?" Still no response. So he decided to take matters into his own hands and began to climb the fence. As he got to the top and was about to heave himself into the man's yard, out came two ferocious and hungry dogs, snarling and barking. He caught himself just in time and jumped back onto the course.

We could see through the gate as the two dogs stopped short of the fence and saw the club dangling from the patio roof. While the homeowner stood motionless, the dogs began to jump and rip at the grip of the club, just within reach. The golfer was beside himself. He knew it was only a matter of minutes before his club would be mangled. We decided it was time to continue play as he ran off to the clubhouse to enlist the help of a marshal. The golf police were his last resort. As we continued up the fairway, we glanced back one last time and watched in amazement as the two Rottweilers began to shred his grip. They probably ate the shaft, too, leaving the homeowner with a 300 cc titanium club head as a dandy toilet float.

Later on that day as we were finishing the round, the marshal, who had tried to help our friend, told us that the homeowner refused to come out and the last he heard, the intrepid golfer was going to the police department to have a real cop accompany him to the house.

Stumped for something to say? Here are some phrases to keep you from yelling, screaming, and otherwise displaying bad manners when you hit a truly atrocious shot (and to give you a good excuse for your ugly play):

- "I should have warmed up."
- "I looked up—again."
- "Every time I take a lesson before I play, this happens."

- "My clubs are in the shop getting fitted. I borrowed these clubs from a very short friend."
- "Yikes!"
- "These new gloves are too tight."
- "These new shoes are killing my feet."
- "Shouldn't have eaten that enchilada for breakfast."
- "The sun was in my eyes."
- "What a crappy lie. My ball was in a small grave."
- "Swung too fast."
- "Swung too slow."
- "Lifted my head again."
- "Shouldn't have had that fifth martini last night."

Temper, Temper, Temper

A bad temper accompanied me during most of my early play. I've pretty much gotten over it, but I did have a run-in several years ago with a ball-washing machine. A particularly bad string of holes, after one of my better starts, infuriated me and I punched the machine with my fist, thinking it was plastic. It turned out to be steel, and I ended up with a compound fracture of the metacarpal (long) bone in my right hand behind my pinky finger. Doctors see this routinely, usually as the result of a barroom brawl. It's called, appropriately, a boxer's break.

My hand immediately went numb, and since I wear gloves on both hands, I didn't see the swelling or dark purple color emerging. Since I hadn't really hit the ball machine that hard, I figured it was just sore and sprained. Not wanting my three partners, who were total strangers, to know how stupid I was, we continued play as if nothing had happened.

There were three holes left to play, and on my next drive I nearly came out of my shoes as I brought the club around and a searing pain shot up my arm. Managing to get the shot off, I realized that if I held the club normally but with only my thumb and the first two fingers of my right hand leaving the last two digits to dangle in midair, I could manage. Unbelievably, I finished par, par, and bogey for a total round of 88, one of my best to that date. Instead of worrying whether my hand was broken or not, I thought maybe I had discovered a new grip. Thinking to myself, "Maybe all those golf gurus are right. I've been using way too much grip pressure. By golly, I'll use my new three-fingered grip tomorrow."

As you might imagine, "tomorrow" did not turn out to be another golf day, nor did the next tomorrow or about 88 tomorrows after that. Living in a cast and not being able to play golf actually turned out quite well. The self-imposed, 12-week hiatus gave me plenty of time to learn to calm down, and it was during that time that I began this book. Every cloud has a silver lining.

Tour professional Curtis Strange feels that high emotions are a sign of high potential, an indicator of passion for the game. Others say discipline and an even temper are the signs of a mature player. I think that everyone seethes inside when things go bad; some are just better than others at disguising their outward reactions.

Bob Hope once told this story about golf rage. "I get upset about bad shots just like everyone else. It's ridiculous to let the game get to us. When I miss a shot I just think about what a beautiful day it is and what pure fresh air I'm breathing. Then I take a deep breath. I do this to give me the energy to break my club."

Playing Alone

After relating a recent golf experience to a fellow player I was asked, "Don't you think that was rude?" I didn't have an answer at the time, but I do now. The round in question was one played at a beautiful course in Sedona, Arizona. Playing as a single off the wait list, I was paired with a surgeon accompanied by his 12-year-old son, who was not playing, and a salesman accompanied by his girlfriend, who also was not participating. All were agreeable sorts. The course was immaculate and the surrounding area strikingly beautiful. Everything was going well, and I had the feeling that I was going to have one of those truly great rounds of golf.

Although I could tell the salesman was probably a much better golfer than the round he was playing, he nevertheless kept quiet about his missed hits and bad luck until we reached the 7th hole. It was a 185-yard, par-3 with deep bunkers to the right and left of the hole. The salesman promptly pulled his tee shot into the left bunker. As we reached the green he was away, and we could see he had a nasty lie buried under the backside lip. His next shot popped straight up and then fell back down into the bunker. From that point on it was all downhill. He finally struggled to an 8, and as he left the green he heaved his club at a tree. I could see the eggs in his pot were really starting to boil.

The surgeon and I were first and second up at the next hole and then the salesman came up to bat. He promptly shanked his ball dead right into some bushes, whereupon he immediately and violently broke his 3-iron over his knee and threw the two pieces off into the scrub. As he went looking for his ball, the surgeon and I passed his girlfriend sitting in the cart. She looked at us and cringed. "I'm sorry. I hate it when he gets this way," she said. "Don't apologize," we both echoed. "It happens to all of us at some time or another." All I could think about was my punching out the ball machine and how ridiculous I must have appeared to my playmates.

As we drove off to the next tee, the salesman was still looking for his ball. Finding it, he ran to catch up with us. Funny thing though—he spent 4 or 5 minutes looking for his ball but never bothered to search for the $150 3-iron. He could have at least saved the head for a new shaft.

On the 8th hole, the surgeon told me that he would have to leave after the 9th because he had custody of his two boys only 5 days out of the month and this was their visiting time. His boy was bored and he felt very guilty. Up to this point he had been shooting bogey golf. At the 10th hole, however, the surgeon continued to play and the salesman got more and more angry. At this point, I overheard a conversation between the boy and his father. As the surgeon apologized and begged for just one more hole, the boy responded, "As long as you can shoot par we can stay." With that challenge the surgeon began to shine. He played par golf for the next three holes.

At the 13th tee, the salesman abruptly quit in frustration and left the course with a mumbled apology and a half-hearted wave. The surgeon, overcome with guilt, came over to me and said, "I really have to go too and spend some time with my son. I'm sorry, and wouldn't you know it, this was going to be the best back nine of my life."

Suddenly, there I was, all alone on the 15th tee with four more holes to play by myself. It was an odd and interesting feeling, kind of Zenlike. No one there to witness my brilliant drives, deft chipping, or deadly putting. Of course, there would be no one there to witness my shanked wedges, chunked chip shots, or sculled long irons. Should I give me some gimmies, or a mulligan or two? Should I hit a few practice drives on each hole and select which one I want to call my real shot? Should I traipse 90 feet up to the pin, pull it, and then walk all the way back to my ball and putt, or should I just fudge a little and leave the stick in all the way?

I decided to have fun. Since the group in front of me was playing at a snail's pace and there wasn't a group behind me, I hit a few mulligan drives on each hole, practiced my pitching and putting around the greens, enjoyed the warm summer day, and left all the pins in. It didn't matter, I had put my scorecard away and I still 3 putted, even with the pins in.

Etiquette Epilogue

As to whether the guys who left were rude or not, I've decided the etiquette should be this: If you're sick, you can leave and not offend. If you need to spend more time with your kid, you can leave and not offend, although maybe you should consider that before getting started in the first place. If you're just having a miserable round, by all means you should stay. Besides having plenty of more chances to improve, you can just consider it a practice round. Leaving would be like Ken Griffey Jr.'s walking off the field after the 4th inning because he struck out twice. There's no better place to practice than on a course. Put away the scorecard and concentrate on making shots one at a time.

How to Drive a Golf Cart

The golf cart was invented in 1940, relatively late to the game of golf but early to the auto industry. Carts were originally intended only for people with disabilities. I guess that accounts for why we all drive them now.

Today the argument looms: to walk or ride? Many push for a walk as it is more akin to what the golf gods intended. Others who own golf courses and therefore rely on the income from cart rentals argue for riding because it speeds up play and allows more folks to visit the cash register each day. It's estimated that carts are used for nearly two-thirds of all 18-hole rounds. That's a lot of carts. As with everything else in golf, there are as many rules and manners involved in carts as there are in play.

In a 1984 U.S. Open qualifying round, Roger Maltbie rented a golf cart. Thinking the USGA had relaxed its regular ban on carts during events, he drove past an official on the first tee. After he had passed an official at the 9th hole, he had already accrued 12 penalty shots.

The next time you use a cart, you may notice some of these thoughts posted on the dashboard. These rules are simple and would appear to be plain old common sense, but the golf gods leave nothing to chance:

- If you're going to drive the cart, sit in the driver's seat, not in the passenger's seat and not in the basket in the back.
- Be sure your passenger is seated and not about to step into or out of the cart.
- Keep all four tires on the ground at all times. It's okay to slide to a stop on occasion, but don't make a habit of hotdogging. The golf cart is not a go-cart.
- Follow the 90-degree rule. That means you can enter the fairway only in a line that's perpendicular to the cart path and drive directly to your ball. It doesn't mean you can drive all over the fairways when the temperature's over 90 degrees.
- Don't pick up hitch-hikers. Carts are for two.
- Don't drive drunk.
- Never back up when someone is about to putt, to tee off, or is otherwise trying to concentrate on a shot. That little back-up beeping noise is extremely irritating.
- Don't use a cart to hide from lightning.

When you're finished playing and you return the cart to the club-house, take all your cigar butts, cigarette packs, sandwich wrappers, beer cans, chewing gum and candy wrappers, soda bottles, and other miscellaneous garbage out first, and don't forget your balls, wallet, scorecard, clubs, shoes, keys, and club head covers.

Tips on Manners

We have only covered a few of the complicated, unwritten rules of etiquette in this chapter. There are hundreds more. And the more you play, the more you'll learn. However, these are the most common courtesies to think about:

- Don't talk when someone is getting ready to hit the ball, and don't ever yell, "Hurry up, we need to finish by Friday."
- Don't play with the ball-cleaning machine while someone is getting ready to hit.
- Don't talk on your cell phone under any circumstances or take a pager with you on the course.
- Make sure everyone in your group is behind you before you hit your ball.
- Keep up with the group in front of you and don't stand on the fairway 270 yards from them if you know you can only hit the ball 190 yards at best.
- Don't ever give advice if it's not asked for, especially to your wife or girlfriend.
- If you're the first to putt out, back off and watch everyone else finish their putts and pretend to be interested.
- Help the greenskeeper and your fellow players by cleaning up the course when you can. Repair at least one ball mark in addition to your own on the green.
- Replace all your divots or repair them with sand and seed (and even one or two that aren't yours). You'll get brownie points from the golf gods that will come in handy some day.
- Identify your ball with a special mark all your own. Be creative. Don't use three dots or an "X"; those have already been thought of.
- The most infuriating and most common discourtesy is players who hold up play by looking for lost balls for hours. Do not ever, under any circumstances, look for a ball for more than 3 minutes. And don't be one of the nuisances who scour the hillsides looking for free balls while waiting for everyone else

to hit. Do not ever use one of the ball scoopers for water hazards. You lost it; live with it.

- Don't step in another player's line, even though most of us are wearing soft spikes and there have already been 500 players who have traipsed and trampled all over the entire green before you have arrived.
- Don't dig your ball out of the cup with your putter.

— CHAPTER 10 —

SO, YOU WANNA BE A MARSHAL?

Marshals have pretty simple jobs. Their primary focus is to ensure that you play the game at breakneck speed. I know this sounds strange. We all think of golf as a leisurely pursuit, a transcendental experience that means communing with and enjoying the great outdoors. But this, like so many other things in golf, is an illusion.

A Career with the Golf Police

A golf marshal must have certain qualities and the proper personal history to be considered for this important job. First and foremost, he must be almost as cranky as a starter. This isn't easy, as golf starters are renowned the world over for their crappy dispositions. Second, a golf marshal must prove that his mother never allowed him to ride go-carts when he was a kid. This pent-up frustration is usually a precursor to a career as a golf marshal.

It is also quite helpful if a future marshal is adept at lecturing children on sinful behavior. To the golf cop, we are all just a bunch of kids running around, playing stick ball, ruining his lawn, and having entirely too much fun.

The Golf Police Are Never There When You Need Them and Are Always There When You Don't

Think back to the last time your foursome was playing behind a group of true novices. They moved like molasses in January on the north side of a glacier. None of them ever broke 100 honestly, and not one of them can drive the ball farther than the women's tee. When they finally do get out to the 250-yard mark—9 shots later—they wait for the equally inept group in front of them to get off the green, which is still 300 yards away.

Where are the speed-it-up police? There's not one to be found. After the slowpokes finally do hit their second shots, you tee off and come marching up behind them once again. This time, they are all looking for their balls or arguing over which ball belongs to whom, since they all are using the same Maxfli 3 brand and none of them took the time to mark their ball. But where is the marshal?

Now, fast forward to the 13th hole. The 90-degree rule is in effect at this course, which means you can take the cart out to your ball only at a 90-degree angle from the cart path (not zigzag all over the beautiful fairways).

Since the marshal hasn't been available all day to help you hustle the novices in front of you or to get them to let you play through, you decide to take your cart on a little shortcut that's not exactly 90 degrees from the path. In fact, you're driving your cart almost right up to the edge of the green, in a brief lapse of etiquette. Bingo! There he is instantly, out of nowhere—like Peter Sellers sneaking up on his faithful houseboy Kato in an old Inspector Clouseau movie. He was hiding behind a tree all day, waiting for just this moment. You're busted, and you feel like a schmuck because you've been a victim all day, and now you're getting lectured for being an even bigger jerk than the guys in front of you.

The marshal has another important job in addition to being the cart traffic cop. He must make sure that everyone wears a "collared" shirt. The marshal is usually a volunteer and he feels you should appreciate his sacrifice. Marshals feel they are kind of like chaperons for all us ill-mannered kids who have come to his prom.

Staying One Step Ahead of the Marshal

The only way to stay ahead of the marshal is to play as fast as humanly possible. One very exaggerated, but true, example of speedy play is 61-year-old Nobby Orens, a 16 handicapper. Nobby flew 10,000 miles to play 18 holes in New York and 18 holes in Hawaii in the same day! He started out shooting a very quick 84 at Clearview

Golf Course in New York, then rushed to the airport, caught the 9:15 A.M. flight to Los Angeles, and, after a 2-hour layover, flew to Honolulu, landing at 4:40 P.M. Orens then took a charter helicopter to Ko Olina Golf Club on Oahu. An hour and 40 minutes later, he carded a 94; he attributed his higher score to jet lag and too many Bloody Marys. And I'll bet you a $1,000 he never once was asked by the marshal to catch up with the group in front of him.

Others like Oren have taken the need for speed perhaps a little too seriously. The fastest 18-hole round played with a single ball was played in 11 minutes! This occurred at the Stonecreek Golf Club in Paradise Valley, Arizona. Members of the club stationed themselves at intervals from the 1st tee to the 18th green and, in relay fashion, hit the ball around the 6,500-yard course. There was only one rule: if a ball went into a hazard, it was abandoned and the round had to be started over. Eventually, after 49 attempts, they managed to complete the course with a single ball.

Now we have "extreme golf," wherein participants attempt to complete 18 holes of golf in less than 45 minutes. This new "sport" is not the result of trying to stay ahead of the marshal; it's a form of exercise. Players cannot use a cart, and they must hit each shot and finish each hole. When you consider the average golf course is about 6,800 yards, or about 4 miles, you have to conclude that just running from one end to the other would take 40 minutes for a healthy runner (and about 5 hours for a golfer). But when you factor in about 90 golf strokes with the running, this is truly an amazing feat.

Getting a Ticket from the Golf Police

Other than making sure we all have collars on our shirts, scolding us for driving the carts onto the greens, and sternly insisting we stay precisely 225 yards behind the group in front of us, the marshals don't have much else to do. Since they are sort of a golf police force, I think we should label them the official license checkers. "What kind of license?" I can hear you saying to yourself.

Many people will call me an elitist for this idea; however, it is my contention that a player should not be allowed on the course until he or she has an official handicap of no more than 25. This would greatly speed up play, to name just one benefit. In fact, I would lobby for taking this even one step further. Every player should have to obtain a license to play before being allowed on a course. This would be the classic win-win situation for players, manufacturers, and golf course owners. Here is how it would work: A governing body would be set up, consisting of one male and one female professional on the tour, one amateur with a fixed handicap, a marshal, and one nonplayer. The board would issue a license to a golfer only after he or she passed both a written and a physical skills examination. The marshals would be in charge of checking all golfers at the first tee to ensure they were currently licensed.

All persons who purchased any golf equipment would be required to fill out a card, listing their name, address, and phone number. They would then be sent a booklet, listing all the rules of golf and all the rules of etiquette, which would be their study manuals. The whole process would be just like getting a driving license.

While golfers were in their study phase, they would only be allowed to practice on the driving range, and they would have to obtain a "learner's permit" to do that. They could study and practice as long as they liked until they felt they were ready to take the test. The test would consist of 50 pages of questions on the rules of golf and etiquette. Here are a few samples:

Question #1

If you know that you cannot possibly hit the ball farther than 175 yards with any club in your bag, how far back should you be from the group in front of you before you hit your ball? (Circle one)

350 yards

250 yards

185 yards

50 yards

Question #2

If you lost your ball in the rough, how much time can you take trying to find it? (Circle one)

90 minutes

20 minutes, if you can prove it's a new ball

45 seconds

Question #3

What is the purpose of those plastic buckets filled with dirt that hang on each side of the cart? (Circle one)

It's not dirt; it's bird seed for you to feed the birdies.

That's where you put out your cigars.

They are stabilizing weights to keep the cart from tipping over when I'm hotdogging it around a tight curve.

It's sand and seed to repair divots.

Put down your pencils. You have completed your test.

A passing grade would be 99 percent correct. If test takers scored 98 percent or less, they would be required to go back to using their learner's permit for another 6 months before retaking the test. Potential golfers would only be allowed two test chances. If they fail the second one, their learner's permit would be revoked for 1 year; the only way to get it back would be to volunteer as a marshal's assistant for 40 hours a week for 6 months at a local municipal course.

The second part of the test would be a live demonstration of skills on the driving range. Golfers would be required to clearly demonstrate that they would be equal to those players with a handicap of 25 or less. Some sample skills would include

- the ability to hit the ball with the head of the club
- the ability to line up and take a putting stroke at the hole in no more than 60 seconds
- the ability to find and wear two matching socks
- the ability to tell which club is a driver and which is a wedge while blindfolded

Having successfully passed both portions of the test, golfers would be issued a license that would be good for life or until their handicap rose above 25 at any time before reaching 98 years of age.

This way the marshals would actually have something to do. They would be issued ticket books so they could cite golfers for rule and etiquette infractions. Marshals could give tickets for such offenses as using a collapsible aluminum pole with a little basket on the end for retrieving balls from ponds. If the pole was in the offender's bag and the golfer wasn't actually caught using it, the fine would be $100. If, on the other hand, the offender was caught using it to scoop a ball out of the pond, the fine would be $500. All fines would have to be paid before the golfer would be allowed to play another round.

The game would go much faster for all of us; there wouldn't be 3-hour waits to get on the course; and profits from the licensing, testing, and ticketing could go into a giant golf lottery every year. Everyone who had a license would be eligible for one free ticket in a national golf lottery. A marshal would retrieve the lucky number from the bowl and the winner would get all the loot. A portion could also be set aside for a marshal's pension and disability program.

My idea about licensing players grew out of an argument I had with my ladyfriend. After making a joke about the idea, she took me seriously and accused me of being a snob. She was just learning to play and resented my idea because it would keep her off the course for probably another 10 years—maybe forever. Three weeks after writing this chapter, I read in *Golf Digest* that some countries have already instituted my idea, to a degree. Fifteen years ago in Sweden, they began to issue a *Grona Kortet* (green card) through a test. If a golfer passed, he or she was allowed to play on the courses; if not, it was back to the range. They don't have an etiquette portion of the Swedish test, which I think is unfortunate, but they do require that you caddy for a round, and, when you begin playing, you're automatically given a starting handicap of 54. Austria, Belgium, France, Germany, and Holland have all followed suit. Apparently, I'm not as crazy as I thought—nor as original.

Cop tips

As in the real world, there are good and bad ways of dealing with the law:

- As much as you'd like to play bumper cars with the marshal, under no circumstances should you anger him. He's old and cranky, but he can get you thrown off the course.

- Make sure you complain about the group in front of you right from the get go to take attention away from your own lapses in etiquette.
- Don't wave and smile when you see the marshal approaching; he'll just think you're up to something.

CHAPTER 11

WHEN ALL ELSE FAILS, CHEAT

Are you honest? Of course you are, but that only applies to real life. It has nothing to do with golf. There is an old saying that goes, "The fastest cart gets the best lie." This means if Hank has any doubts as to the position of his ball for his next shot, he better get out there ahead of everyone else so he won't be seen "improving" his lie with the old foot wedge.

There isn't a golfer on earth—professional or hacker—who hasn't technically cheated. But, of course, that's because the rules aren't fair to begin with. In fact, when the golf gods were young, there was no such thing as an unplayable lie. Think about that the next time you're out in the cabbage.

Honesty and integrity are the backbones of the game. Like the godfather in mafia movies always says to the best friend he has to whack, "I love ya like a son, but we all gotta follow the rules. It's the only thing that keeps us in business."

Technically, golf is a game of skill built upon a foundation of honesty and ethics because there are no referees or umpires to supervise the players. That's one of the lures of the game. Where did all the honesty and ethics come from? Actually, it was a Greek statesman named Plenides who first brought the concept of morality and ethics before the Senate. Plenides said, "To lead a moral and ethical life, do more than is expected of you, and less than you are allowed." He was promptly stabbed to death. He's one of the golf gods now; he's in charge of the rules and is known as "Plenti-o-strokes."

Because of the need for speed and because we want to maintain some social decorum and keep our friends, we fudge. Take, for instance, this rule: If two people were to hit the identical brand of ball into nearly the same spot on the fairway, and neither could determine whose ball is whose, they must both promptly proceed back to the tee and start over, taking a penalty in the bargain for having lost their balls. This rule is definitely not going to speed up play and so, in the interest of having a good day, we just decide which ball each player will hit and continue.

The USGA takes the rules far more seriously than most sports ruling bodies. There are 34 rules for this simple game and more than 200 pages of decisions that affect those rules. In baseball, the second baseman rarely touches the bag on a double play. In basketball, the stars are penalized far less than the average players, and fouls are called against opponents who so much as breathe too close to them under the basket. In golf, no infractions are ignored, no heads are turned, and no leniencies are considered by the officials.

Here are a few astounding invocations of golf rules:

- Steve Elkington once picked a piece of grass to chew on and was assessed a 2-stroke penalty for touching the ground around a hazard. (Someone must really have disliked him.)

- In 1970, Raymond Floyd wrote his front-side total of 36 in the 9-hole box instead of the box reserved for the total of all nine holes and turned it in. He shot a 38 on the back and had to post a total of 110.

- In a 1971 Ryder Cup match, Arnold Palmer replied to an opponent's caddie's question, "Gosh, what did you hit there, Mr. Palmer?" "A 5-iron" was his answer. Although the match play hole was halved, it was later awarded to Palmer and the Americans as a penalty to the opposition for seeking illegal advice. You are not allowed to ask a partner or an opponent which club he has used, but it's okay to answer.

- An incident involving Denis Watson in the 1985 U.S. Open at Oakland Hills led to a new ruling. After Watson's putt, his ball clung to the edge of the hole by less than the width of a whisker. At the time, the ruling stated that if a ball didn't drop into the hole within a maximum of 10 seconds after arrival, it must be putted out. Watson waited a little more than 10 seconds and his ball did indeed finally drop in on its own. He was assessed a 2-stroke penalty and awarded a 6 instead of a 4. The rule now says that if a player waits more than 10 seconds and the ball then falls into the hole, the player has indeed holed out but must add 1 penalty stroke to his score, essentially making a tap in or a wait the same.

Sometimes interpretation of the rules gets muddy. The PGA does not allow carts with the exception of the recent court decision that compelled them to let Casey Martin ride because of his disability. Yet there aren't any rules against bringing your own chair. In a 1957 U.S. Open, Dick Mayer, in his duel with Cary Middlecoff, brought a stool with him and sat down and rested each time Middlecoff prepared to hit his shots. Mayer won with a final round of 72 to Middlecoff's 79.

There are several differences between the USGA and the USWG (us weekend golfers): On the tour, every shot must be completed. There are no gimmies or mulligans. In the universal need to speed up play on your local municipal course, everyone takes license with the rules. One of the most oft-repeated infractions is not holing out our putts. "Come on, that's a gimmie. We gotta go. Those four guys behind us who threw a ball at you on the last hole are gaining on us."

Not taking the time to hole out your putt, even in the interest of speedy play, is, in my humble opinion, a loss. I think it's fun to go through the motion, even if it's only a 6-incher, just to hear that beautiful plunking sound as your ball finally arrives at its intended destination. After all, it's been a long trip. The sound of the ball falling into the cup is second only to the heavenly sound of a great drive where your ball meets the sweet spot on one of those big titanium drivers.

"Play It As It Lies" and Other Absurdities

Here's a purely hypothetical scenario: You're playing a round with two pals who are betting heavily on each hole. The first of them—we'll call him Al—tees off and then jumps into his cart to wait for his friend—we'll call him Hank—to tee off. After Hank hits his ball, Al puts the pedal to the metal and is off in his own cart to the right rough to find his ball. Aha! There it is in that little clump of fescue, a particularly gnarly grass intended to make the rough, *very* rough. His ball is all nestled down warm and snug, only one dimple visible. Al's stuck just behind a tree—only a few inches—but, nevertheless, behind a tree.

Not wanting to start his day off on the wrong note, Al quickly glances back at the group to see just where everyone is. He's fortunate, you're all doing the same thing—looking for your balls in the rough and not looking his way, so he gives his ball the old foot wedge and nudges it out just a bit to clear the tree.

Hank doesn't notice because he's using his own foot wedge on the other side of the fairway. As your group approaches the green, both Al and Hank hit their balls past the green onto the backside where neither can see each other. Al is prepared. He's got a ball in his pocket just like the one he started with, just in case he can't find the one he sculled past the green. Sure enough, it's nowhere to be found, so he discreetly lets his second ball slip through the hole in his pocket that he's conveniently prepared for just such a moment. Voila! Now it's just a nice pitch to the green instead of an out-of-bounds-penalty stroke.

As Al is quietly pitching his ball, Hank has found himself in a deep bunker on the other side—so deep that no one approaching can see him. He's not going to leave anything to chance and lose $5, so he crouches down low, uses the hand wedge, grabs a fistful of sand along with his ball, and gives it the old underhand pitch perfectly up to about 8 inches from the hole. Al's ball arrives nearly as ideally, just about 10 inches out. Then they both miss their putts.

By now you're thinking, "Boy, this guy sure knows a lot about cheating. I don't know if I'd ever want to play with him." Nah, I don't cheat—much. I see it and read about it though. For example, in a 1971 Colonial Invitational tournament, Dave Hill was not having fun. He was spraying his shots everywhere. On the 12th hole his ball found a bunker. Known as temperamental, he stormed into the bunker, and to the astonishment of the gallery, picked up his ball, and threw it up on the green. He was, of course, disqualified and fined, but he didn't care. He told the press, "I've always wanted to try throwing the ball at the hole." Apparently he wanted out of the tournament anyway.

Using the Cart to Your Advantage

Back to Al and Hank, who don't miss an opportunity to get a leg up on each other. Al is particularly adept at using the cart to his advantage in a number of ways, starting with his insistence on always being the driver. A driver has distinct advantages over a rider.

If you plan on a little subterfuge with your betting friends, make sure you drive the cart. You can ensure this by racing out to the cart and placing your clubs on the driver's side first. If your buddy beats you to it, you can surreptitiously loosen the strap on his bag while he's teeing off at the first hole. When he stomps on the accelerator and you head out to your balls, his bag will fall off the cart. Immediately offer to remedy the situation. This will give you the opportunity to switch bags and put yours on the driver's side. After about three holes of bumping into each other, trying to get to your bag on the opposite side of the cart, you can suggest firmly that you drive. This can come in very handy.

Here are several scenarios where a cart can be used to its best advantage:

- Because Al's and Hank's balls are about the same distance from the hole and both golfers are getting out of the cart at the same time, Al can position the cart between his ball and Hank's. Since Al is driving, he parks the cart closer to his ball to save him walking distance, and more importantly, to keep Hank from seeing his ball. This allows Al a slight improvement in ball position.

- As Hank is about to step up to his next shot, Al positions the cart 6 inches behind Hank's backswing. If Al is really lucky, the sun will cast a deep shadow across half of Hank's ball, making it difficult to see. And then, just for good measure, as Hank is about to hit, Al can make the apologetic gesture of putting the cart in reverse so it makes that irritating beeping noise.

- When Hank's and Al's balls are both off the fairway and not visible, even if Al knows where Hank's ball is, Al is always sure to drop Hank off to look for his ball first without letting him take a club out of his bag. Al then races off to find his own ball. Once he's located it, he drives back to Hank, but only half way. Hank takes two or three clubs out of his bag, because he can't be sure which one he'll need, and then must trek back to his ball, giving Al ample time to use the cart to block Hank's view of Al improving his lie.

If you are cunning, you can help your opponent defeat himself, especially when there's money involved. Sneezing, coughing, and belching are all within fair bounds during the putt or the drive. Moaning, groaning, and an overanimated rolling of one's eyes can also be unnerving. Humorist Dave Barry wrote, "Few pleasures on earth match the feeling that comes from making a loud bodily function noise just as a guy is about to putt."

The volatile Tommy Bolt, known more for throwing clubs and tantrums, was actually fined once for farting! At the 1959 Memphis

Invitational Open, as he waited for one of the other players to putt, Bolt released a blast so thunderous that most of the entire gallery broke into collective laughter. Not everyone thought it was so funny though, including a few of the players, and one of the spectators was so offended that he reported Bolt to the officials, who fined Tommy $250 (a lot of money at the time). He insisted it was an accident and couldn't be helped but got no relief. When queried on the incident by the press, Bolt responded, "That story got blown out of proportion."

Playing the exact same ball as your opponent can sometimes shave as many as 5 strokes off your score, depending upon your cart management skills. Again, the fastest cart will get the best lie, but if you are going to claim your partner's ball instead of your own feeble hit, you must use an identical ball and at least hit on the same side of the course as he has. Of course, to ensure you have the same ball, you must carry at least 3 each of all the top 10 most popular balls. If your opponent has been smart enough to identify his balls with some clever design, this strategy probably will not work.

Most honest players are concerned with their course management skills and overlook the importance of "scorecard management." This is another important reason to be the driver—since the scorecard is always kept on the steering wheel. Here is another unique opportunity to pick up some strokes on your opponent. Wait a few holes before you write down your score. This will allow for short-term memory loss, and as he will undoubtedly be concentrating on his own game, your opponent won't remember what you scored three holes back. Some courses actually supply you with pencils that have erasers; this obviously presents yet another opportunity for creative scorekeeping. Remember not to press too hard though when entering your first score.

Taking liberties with your handicap can also be very helpful in matches where wagers are substantial. The game of golf is so honest that you're actually allowed to post your own scores on the computer in the pro shop after each round. Since all amateur tournaments and most wagering are conducted using the handicapping index, it's easy to see how some people, especially those who don't type well, may inadvertently push the wrong keys on the computer.

Once you've obtained your handicap, you can then conveniently forget to post any good rounds you may be lucky enough to have, thus raising your published handicap. The USGA officials in charge of tallying all the scores always take the highest 10 rounds off your record each month. This is supposed to keep people from cheating. How many guys do you know in your club who post their best scores? Many players just keep entering inflated scores after each round, or they just don't record a particularly good round. If a player is truly a 10 handicap, he would add that number to the standard par for a course, usually 72, so you would expect him to shoot about an 82. If he has always entered only high scores, his published handicap might be more like an 18 instead of his real 10. In a tournament this player would deduct 18 strokes off his actual gross score. If he truly is a 10 and has shot 82 that day, instead of awarding him a fair net—or 82 minus 10 for a 72—they would award him a 64 (his real score of 82 minus his fake handicap of 18).

Beware of using this tactic when betting, though. The golf gods have already accounted for this behavior. They make sure you're playing with someone else who has artificially raised his handicap, thus rendering the two of you evenly matched after all.

Playing by the Rules

Call it "winter rules." Call it "friendly play." Call it a "gimmie," a "mulligan," or a "do-over." Call it whatever you like, but everyone has fudged somewhere, sometime. I read an article the other day that reported that one of the top female players in the world was seen attending a seminar on the rules of golf. This makes it clear to me that no one knows what the rules are to begin with.

With regard to rule 13-2, which deals with the subject of improving your lie, this rule basically says that you are not allowed to improve your lie, or position of your ball, by breaking, twisting, or bending anything around you, such as tree branches and the like. There is an exception though, as there is for most of the rules. (It's the exceptions that make the rule book so long.) This exception allows for any action that may occur as you fairly take your stance. For instance, if your backswing takes out a tree limb but you still continue your stroke through the ball, it's okay.

The key words here are "as may occur in fairly taking his stance." What could possibly happen to that little ball as you "fairly take your stance?" It depends on where everyone else is looking.

Apparently, the notion of playing fast with the golf rules has quite a history. According to the magazine *Living Age*, June 5, 1897,

> It is the commonly accepted belief that the vast majority of players belong to a class which is incapable of cheating. I am sorry to have to express the deliberate conviction that the belief in the honor and honesty of golfers has a very unsubstantial foundation in fact. I have golfed for a number of years over all kinds of greens, and with all sorts of people; and on innumerable occasions I have been driven to strongly suspect my opponent of cheating, and on many occasions, I have positively detected him doing so.

Add this from the *New York Times,* June 20, 1897,

> The USGA Special Committee has made no change in the words of the rules as they stand from the Royal and Ancient Golf Club of St. Andrews, Scotland, but they have appended said rules of the United States

> Golf Association to whit: Rule 11. Ice, snow, or hail
> within a club-length of the ball through the green may
> be removed, but on the putting green only by brush-
> ing slightly with the hand, and only across the putt
> and not along it.

Apparently so-called snow golf rules were being employed at Lakewood and Baltrusol during the winter one year. When snow covered the greens, many of the players actually made grooves with their clubs straight to the hole so that the ball could virtually be bowled into the cup.

Of course Hank and Al don't care much for the rules, the golf gods, or the PGA, but the rules, as arcane and complicated as they are, still help make the game what it is. The PGA takes them very seriously. Take, for example, the infamous case of Craig Stadler. A few years ago, he was playing the 14th hole at Torrey Pines in San Diego in a tour event. His ball came to rest under a tree that was surrounded by mud. He placed a towel on the ground and used it to kneel on under the low limbs so he wouldn't get his pants dirty. An astute armchair golfer saw this action on television and wrote to the PGA, stating that Stadler was guilty of "building a stance." By kneeling on something, even a towel, he was, in effect, changing his shot and breaking Rule 13-3:"(a player is entitled to place his feet firmly in taking his stance, but shall not build his stance)." The officials had no recourse but to agree and disqualify Stadler. In my opinion, that's being overly attentive to the rules. Technically, it's cheating, but it undoubtedly won't be adhered to by any foursome I know.

Tips on How to Cheat and Bet

Cheating isn't the best way to get ahead, but if you are determined to do so, be careful:

- I've told you about smart cart management, using the shield and backaway techniques. I've described how a strategically placed hole in your pants pocket can do wonders for lowering your score. You've heard about the foot wedge and the hand wedge in action. These are all techniques with which you can directly affect your own score. But how about affecting the scores of your betting and playing buddies? By lowering your score and simultaneously helping your partners to raise theirs, you can really put distance between your games and some dough in your pocket. Just make sure you put it in the pocket without the hole.

- Distraction is the key word. By redirecting the focus of your fellow players, you can enjoy a really low score. Whistling, humming, coughing, sneezing, belching, passing wind, moaning, and other bodily sounds along with gestures like eye rolling are all perfectly legitimate devices intended to break an opponent's concentration and focus.

- Make sure you get the fastest cart, and if you're in the same cart with your opponent, make sure you're the driver and score keeper.

- Always carry extra balls in your pocket for those unfortunate moments when you lose your ball.

- Make up a new game to wager on, one that's so confusing only you know the rules.

- Never bet with a guy who carries a 1- or 2- iron in his bag.

- Never bet with a stranger.

- Look at your partner's left hand. If he has calluses, he's either a farmer or a better golfer than you are.

- If your course doesn't supply pencils with erasers, make sure you have a good supply of your own.

CHAPTER 12

GOLF TALK: THE LANGUAGE OF LOVE

All groups that play, socialize, work, or otherwise congregate together develop their own cryptic shorthand language. It's what helps bind the group together. It keeps outsiders out and insiders in, and it makes everyone feel more important than they really are.

Golf is certainly no different. In fact, there is no better example of a secret language. Birdies, bogeys, par, eagles, gimmies, and mulligans are but a few of the strange words that describe our funny little game.

Some of these terms were coined by the original golf gods who got to golf heaven shortly after the 14th century. Most of them have names like McCavindish or Robert Bruce. They are having the biggest laughs of all the golf gods because they know that most of these words are gibberish and really don't mean a thing.

Like any language, you must listen carefully and study to fully comprehend it. This can take many rounds of golf and a lot of eaves-dropping at the 19th hole. In fact, let's listen in right now as Ralph and Hank are having a beer in the clubhouse and discussing their round.

> Hank: "Man, did you see my drive on the 12th? Came right out of my shoes and banana-sliced it big time into the salad. But even from there, I figure I can get home in 2 with my 8. I'm thinking I'm still gonna be dancing, but no I chili-dipped that one and now I'm lying 3 and I'm still out 130. Left a divot the size of Rhode Island.
>
> Then, on my 3rd, I topped it bad and couldn't hold the linoleum. It skated out the backside into the Sahara with no chance of digging out. I tried twice to scoop it out of the beach. So now I'm lying 5 and I'm still not on the dance floor.

Finally, on my 6th, I'm out of the beach but, of course, I caught the sweet spot big time for the first time all day, and it flew 50 yards over the pin into mulligan lake.

Jeez, now I'm looking at the snowman. So I drop and take out my new 79-degree doorstopper, hoping for the right launch angle. The golf gods must've been smiling cause I got the spin and it did a moondance back across the tile right into the cavity for a niner! Jeez what a hole. Did ya see it, Ralph, did ya?!"

Ralph: "Nah!"

We have our own language, and it's part of the fun. Here are some of my current favorite words and phrases:

Bacon strip—Extremely large divot.

Barber—One who shaves strokes off his scorecard.

A Bo Derek—Scoring a 10 on a hole.

Body bags—Absolutely unplayable lie.

Bogey—One of the most oft-repeated words in the language. The origin of this word is generally attributed to one Major Charles Wellman, who in 1890, was heard to exclaim that the standard par score of the course was "a regular Bogey Man," which referred to a popular song of the time, "Hush, hush, hush, here comes the Bogey Man . . . he'll catch you."

Burglar—A player who deliberately pads his handicap.

A Buzzard—Two over par. Another way of stating double bogey.

Cheerleaders—People who dress in nothing but expensive designer golf clothes.

Clinton putt—A putt that starts left, breaks right, then comes back to the left.

Equalizer—The eraser on the end of your scoring pencil.

Foozle—Originally this meant "to fool around with someone's hair." In golf, foozle came to be known as a badly hit shot.

Frozen rope—A ball that has been hit so straight it can't bend, slice, or hook. Like a real frozen rope, you aren't likely to see any in your near future unless you're a longshoreman working the docks in January.

Golf lawyer—A self-appointed and unwanted rules nitpicker.

Goose pate—Bird droppings on the greens.

A Liz Taylor—A shot that's a little fat, but not all that bad.

Marquis de Sod—A greenskeeper who takes particular delight in difficult pin placements.

A Mick Jagger—A lip-out.

Nugget—A brand new, or nearly new, ball in a basket full of the usual duds at a practice range.

Pre-Mix—A bunker that's so bad, all you have to do is add water and it turns to concrete.

Pucker factor—The relative difficulty of a shot. On a scale of 1 to 10, this shot over that 40-foot-deep bunker has a pucker factor of 9.5.

Road kill—A ball hit into the gallery.

Scalpel—A putter used to extract $5 bills out of opponents' wallets.

Scratch—The term "scratch," as in a good player, comes from 19th-century traces. The "scratch" was a line drawn in the dirt indicating the starting line for a foot race. To help even the differences in the abilities of the runners, handicaps were given by allowing them to start at points in front of the scratch line. Scratch came to mean a 0 handicap and eventually found its way into the golfer's language.

Sweet spot—Mythical area of the clubface located in the duffer's mind.

Swing oil—Alcoholic beverage used to loosen up your swing.

Bail out—Improving a poorly started hole with a great second or third shot or putt. Also referred to as "recovery," which is mostly what you'll be trying to do.

Have fun. Create your own new words. Help enrich the language. It's a relatively new one as languages go, so there's plenty of room for creative thinking. Think how much fun it would be to come up with your own description of a shot or predicament and then hear someone use the same phrase on a course in Japan 6 months later.

Golf Is Like Sex

The language of golf is similar to the language of sex. In fact, both games are quite alike—all the good parts last about 5 seconds, and it takes way too long to get to the good parts.

A recent study showed that most weekend golfers would rather shoot a round of par golf than have sex with a Hollywood star. Personally, that would have to depend on who the star was and what golf course I could shoot par on. If it was a choice between a round at Pebble Beach and sex with an aging starlet, I'd be winding my way up the California coast right now.

Hitting the sweet spot is golf's orgasm, although in golf you have the orgasm first. This occurs when you hit the sweet spot with the head of your driver. Then you have the foreplay. This occurs as you chase your ball all around the course trying to get it into the hole so you can hurry up and get to the next tee and have another orgasm.

The similarities between the two languages are endless:

• Try putting a little more feeling into it.
• It's been so long, I can't remember the last time we played a round.
• Holes, balls, heads, shafts.

- The ball kissed the lip of the hole.
- Damn that is a long one!
- What am I doing wrong?
- Eh gads! Look at how short you are.

Golf was invented by men, what do you expect?

When it comes to swearing, golf talk becomes half sexual and half religious. Also, I've noticed that the actual words uttered are linked directly to the type of bad shot that was made and that most players scream the same phrases in the same situations. For example:

Whereas a putt of more than 25 feet that's missed will solicit only a groan from 99 percent of the weekend players, a putt of less than a foot that's missed is usually followed by a more hardy "damn it." A badly sculled 3-iron from the fairway will result in a protracted "damn it!!#@!!" But a chunked or chili-dipped sand wedge from just 30 yards out will elicit (X@#!!@!!#!) words strong enough to make a rock star blush.

I used to berate myself and use language far worse than I've written here. As a prime example, a couple of years ago I was playing a course in Orange County, California, called Strawberry Farms. Playing with a good friend who occasionally got a kick out of my tirades, I was having a fairly good round and thought I might come in at about 86. That is until the 13th hole, where I had a miserable drive that put me in the deep rough. Eventually, I hacked my way to an 8 on a par 5. The next hole was worse, and I began to swear, at first under my breath and then louder and more vociferously as the round progressed. As I glanced over to my friend standing with the other two players in our group, he was howling and they were sitting wide-eyed with astonishment. I apologized for my profanities and we continued on. The same behavior and events took place on the 15th hole. My friend (who wants to remain nameless for fear the sisters in his church might frown on what he did, not that they will be reading this book) continued to chuckle, but the other two players were stone silent. I continued to swear albeit at a lower decibel level until we arrived at the 17th hole whereupon my friend spoke to the now two silent players and divulged his prank to me for the first time. Apparently, back at the 13th hole where I was really raving, my friend was with the two other players telling them, quite seriously, that I was a Catholic priest and had my own small parish in San Juan Capistrano. He told them I was known as Father Roberto. He was so convincing and my language was so astounding, they were totally aghast, to the point that they couldn't even talk. My swearing would have been bad for a longshoreman, let alone a priest. We all got a hefty laugh when he confessed that it was all a joke.

Origins of the Language

Despite the seemingly random nature of golf jargon, some of the words can actually be traced back to their origins. We know, for example, that the word "caddie" had a royal beginning. In the 16th century, golf, for whatever reason, became the object of royal patronage. King James V was a fan and passed along his love of the sport to his ill-fated daughter, Mary, Queen of Scots.

Mary became an avid golfer. While at school in France, she would play frequently and would have other students carry her clubs. The students were called "cadets," with the French pronunciation being, "cad-day."

Mary's dedication to the game eventually won her disfavor with the church. It seems she played a round a mere 3 days after her husband, Lord Darnley, was murdered. She was subsequently executed.

Mary's story reminds me of a joke. An obsessive golfer takes his wife out to play a round on their 25th anniversary. The guy is a good player with a 3 handicap. The two of them get to the 3rd hole where the husband's second shot has landed behind a small maintenance shed. He's very upset, knowing he'll have to lay up sideways out into the fairway, but his wife comes up with a brilliant idea.

She says to him, "Honey, look! If I hold this door open for you, you might be able to hit it through the door, out that window on the other side, and end up just in front of the green." The husband thinks this is a great idea, so he tells his wife to stand there and hold the door open while he takes deadly aim. Sure enough the husband cracks a big one off, and the ball strikes his wife dead center on the forehead, killing her instantly.

A few weeks later the guy is out on the same course with his buddies. As luck would have it, his second shot on the 3rd hole lands in almost the exact spot as before. As he is surveying his plight, one of his buddies walks up to him and says, "Hey, Ralph, look! I'll bet if I hold this door open for you, you could hit it through the door and out that window in the back and end up just in front of the green!" "Oh no, I'm not doin' that again," he exclaimed. "I tried that last time and I shot a double bogey!"

I Say "Tomayto," You Say "Tomahto"

When I had just begun to play the game, my partners and I had an argument over words on the course. It was a friendly game, meaning we weren't betting or playing in a tournament, so some minor license was being taken in the rules.

All of us were about 10 feet from the hole except for Barbara, whose ball was about 3 feet away. As she began to pick up her ball without putting, she announced, "That's inside the leather." "Wait a minute," one of us exclaimed, and thereafter ensued a lively discussion of just what constitutes "inside the leather."

In friendly games, a putt that's close is considered either a "gimmie," or it's "inside the leather." That afternoon we all agreed that none of us understood the measurement. I took it to mean that any ball that is the same distance from the hole as the length of a club's leather grip is a "gimmie." The others argued that it is the distance measured by placing the head of the putter in the hole and laying it down on the green; the distance from the hole to the lowest point of the leather grip is "inside the leather." There is obviously a big difference in those two distances.

After a little research, I found that the distance in question is measured from the top of the grip—or butt of the club—to the bottom of the grip, approximately 18 inches for the average putter. I'm sure this is great for friendly games, but it seems awfully generous to me.

I've decided there are different invisible distances around the pin, each referring to the level of friendship between the players in the foursome. Since these distances can't be accurately measured with a ruler, I call them regions. There is the gimmie or concession region. This is the bull's-eye, and its radius is about 5 inches out from dead center of the cup. Next comes the region of compromise. Depending on how well you know and like your partner, this can vary from 5 inches to about 18 inches. The region of debate extends to about 23 inches; then comes the region of disharmony followed by the region of "you gotta!"

In the oldest tradition of the game, a player is to strike his ball from exactly where it lies. Period. No dropping, no out-of-bounds, no gimmies, mulligans, or any other shenanigans. It has not been scientifically documented, however, that in polite play among friends a gimmie is where all others in your group agree that your ball is so close to the hole, it would be all but impossible to miss. Everyone knows better, because we've all witnessed botched 3-inch putts. Another term that is used almost as often as "gimmie" is "mulligan."

One of the most common experiences is the "yips" at the first tee of each round of golf. These jitters are usually due to performance anxiety and lack of proper warm up prior to the start of play. All but the real golf veterans get a little nervous on the first big drive. This is particularly true because there are more people watching you on the first tee than at any other time during the round. Doing well is important, so of course, there is a strong possibility you won't. For this reason, and again only amongst very good friends, a mulligan is sometimes awarded. This means you get one more chance to tee it up without it being recorded as an extra stroke on your scorecard.

What these terms have in common is that they all mean you get something you're not supposed to. In the case of a mulligan, you get to leave a stroke off your card. With a gimmie, you still record a stroke; you just don't have to embarrass yourself by maybe adding a couple more. Tradition can now include even a second mulligan per round, beginning on the 10th tee. If you include two mulligans per round and an average of about 4 to 6 strokes of fudging, you can arrive at the average golfer's score of about 94, which is, of course, more like 100, but no one really wants to see three digits on their scorecard. At the end of this book is a glossary of terms that will be helpful in your quest to learn the language of golf.

If you want to be cool, don't try to make up any new words or phrases until you've been playing awhile and have had a chance to absorb a lot of the conversations around you. If you have played the game for more than a few months, you're now hopelessly hooked like the rest of us. It will be difficult not to talk golf with a fellow golfer or even a total stranger when you learn he also plays the game. It's interesting to note that two men can talk for hours about golf, but when they finally run out of golf stories, they discover they have absolutely nothing else in common.

CHAPTER 13

THE DRIVING RANGE: A PLAYGROUND FOR ADULTS

The driving range is a wonderful place, kind of like an amusement park for adults. The range is the only place you can hit things real hard and far without breaking windows or hurting anyone, except maybe yourself.

Golf is just as auditory as it is visual. One of the biggest kicks is the sound and feel of a well-struck shot. The satisfaction of smacking that ball squarely in the middle of the sweet spot—straight and true and long—is one of the key ingredients in forming the addiction.

I can prove my point. Go to any range and look at each of the golfers hitting on the line. Count how many are using drivers or other woods and how many are pitching, chipping, or putting. I guarantee you that 85 percent are swinging for the moon with that big driver—a relentless, no-rest-or-breath-in-between-shots, frantic pounding of the driver. Why? Because when they manage that one sweet shot out of 30, there is no feeling like it. They get the false sense that, since they did it once, they will be able to do it again; and true enough, they will, but not before hitting a wheelbarrow full of balls and forking over $30 to the guy at the counter.

Just think of what a cash cow the ranges must be. Other than the cost of the land, this has got to be the least brain-taxing, highest-margin business in the world. It's simple. Buy some balls, hire a grumpy starter-type of guy to run the cash register and a mindless guy to drive the little tank that grabs all the balls, and you're up and running. People come in droves with cash in hand to hit the same balls over and over again, and the tank commander scoops them up and brings them back to a never ending line of baskets. They don't even have to put much grass on the range. I've practiced at many that have grass only around the yardage-marker pins. And the customers, for the most part, don't even care how bad the balls are because, after all, they're just range balls. Everyone assumes they are going to be bad. Besides, there's no other place to practice.

A Great Playground in the Desert

My all-time favorite driving range is called Cracker Jax, and it's in Scottsdale, Arizona. It has a first and second floor, and from what I've heard, it was modeled after Japanese ranges. A two-deck range makes a lot of sense in Japan, where real estate is at a premium and land sells for $10,000 a square inch.

It is great fun to hit off the upper deck because your ball appears to go farther than when you're hitting on a ground-level range, and it certainly has no trouble getting off the ground. On the ground level of this range there is a great machine at each mat that tees up your ball for you. Think about that for a moment. No more bending over after each shot to grab a ball out of the bucket and place it on the rubber tee. This gesture is not only hard on your back but is difficult to do with a hangover.

At Cracker Jax they give you a plastic card that, depending upon the amount you paid at the counter, gives you a credit of up to 200 balls at a time. You then find an empty mat and insert the card into the machine that is next to each station. The machine credits you with however many balls you paid for and, automatically and magically, up rises a ball on a rubber tee from under the mat. You never have to touch a thing. The height of the tee is determined by pushing a button to tell the machine how many millimeters high or low you want the ball to be.

A wide hose leads from each machine up into a tube, which travels the length of the line and into the pro shop, where balls are fed continuously into the tube, then into the hose, and finally down into each machine. What a great idea! No more lugging buckets of balls from the window to the line, where you invariably lose a few bouncing balls. No more bending over 200 times, losing your rhythm and, if you're over 50, getting back spasms.

The whole setup was such great fun that I hit about 500 balls. I couldn't stop, which is why some smart people invented it. If you don't have to lug balls out to the range and you don't have to bend over all day, you're going to hit more balls in a shorter period of time.

Another bit of fun I discovered was the fast repetition with which I could launch 25 to 30 balls. Instructors tell us that we should spend an hour hitting a basket of balls to fully allow our muscles to memorize the movements. Take it slowly and deliberately is what they suggest, and I agree. However, I conducted a little experiment at Cracker Jax. Noticing that there was about a 3-second lag between when the ball left the tee and the next one popped up and was fully stationary, I decided to set my gun on automatic instead of the manual single-shot mode. Furiously, I pounded each ball as soon as it showed its little white dimples.

Once I hit a ball, the time it took me to fully wind up again and begin my down slash, was just about 2.5 seconds; thus I became an atomic pendulum. As one ball was launched, I was starting my backswing and as the ball appeared so did the head of my driver, and so on until I had to stop and catch my breath.

What was truly amazing was how straight my drives went. You would think this kind of furious and continuous slinging and swinging would produce plenty of slices and shanks, but it was just the opposite. My mind didn't have time for swing thoughts or analysis. For the first time ever, my swing was pure muscle memory: instinctive weight shift, smooth as silk, Michael Jordanesque, born-with-it fluid.

My weight shifted easily from back to front, like a home-run batter who winds up like a dishrag and pushes off the back side with a vengeance. The more balls I hit, the more I wanted to hit, until my fuel tank went empty and my hands went numb. It was exhilarating!

"Practice Makes Perfect"

Greg Norman wrote these words to me in answer to a letter I sent him asking for advice. He was wrong. We never perfect the game of golf. If we did, it wouldn't be any fun. I think practice makes permanent, maybe. Whatever you practice diligently will become a part of your game. This has recently been proven by sports physiologists who have studied muscle memory. These experts suggest that after you've practiced you should not play or go back out and practice again for at least 8 hours or longer. That's the minimum time it takes for your muscles to learn their lessons. Once that swing, good or bad, has had a chance to settle into the tiny minds of your muscles, it's there to stay—or at least temporarily.

The range is obviously the only real place to practice. I know this because everyone, my teacher included, tells me not to practice while I'm playing on the course. They tell me to "trust my swing." Boy, what a leap of faith that is. So you must go to the range and hit lots and lots of balls to develop a swing you can trust. It is said that Ben Hogan hit balls until his hands bled. I like to practice, but that might be a little aggressive for me. Have you ever considered that maybe Hogan didn't have any natural talent and the only way he was able to play as well as he did was to practice 23-1/2 hours a day?

Like a relationship, the swing is part mechanical and part feel, and it takes a fair amount of time to develop your swing to a level of trust. In the beginning, of course, there is nothing to trust and that is why we all play so poorly. So now that I've got a swing I can trust, why am I still playing so poorly?

Everything about playing the game is ritualistic. All the sports gurus tell us to develop a routine when we practice and before each and every shot when we're playing. Visiting the driving range is kind of a routine, too, and if the one you visit is anything like the one I go to, it is a small social village of sorts. There is a putting green that's rarely open because they don't want to spoil the nice flat green surface.

My range is kind of seedy and there is a grumpy starter-type guy who disagreeably hands out baskets of balls, just like on the course. Even if it's an automated range, they still have a grumpy guy who sells the plastic cards or odd-shaped tokens to put into the machines to get the balls.

Profits on the Range

Like my favorite range, yours may also have a bar. Unless it's a high-end practice facility, these bars usually cater to the real salt-of-the-earth players and even to people who never play golf but just like to hang out in dimly lit, funky bars. Usually the decor is 1950s bowling alley motif. When you walk in, it's hard to recognize anyone because the heavy cloud of smoke that envelops the entire lounge hangs at just about neck level, so when you're standing and all the patrons are sitting, all you can see are their knees. The bartender is invariably a case-hardened veteran. She has only three teeth in her head and a plug of chaw in her cheek, and she looks like Tug Boat Annie. If you order a drink when she's in the middle of a game of dice with the bar flies, she'll shoot you an evil eye that will send a chill up your spine. Eventually, if you're really patient and polite, you'll be able to get her attention for a warm beer.

Range Routine

You should have a routine at the range similar to the routine that instructors tell us we should have on the course before each shot. My routine usually starts with an argument with the guy who hands out the buckets of balls.

After I've paid for my balls, I begin looking for the best mat, one with some substance still left in it. What I'm looking for is the one mat on the range that's thick, plump, and juicy. Most of the mats are as thin as cheap potato chips. The only part left that's thick enough to hit balls off of is about 2 inches of outer edge, where no iron has ever ventured. These mats look like a mattress a sumo wrestler slept on for 15 years without ever getting out of bed.

Part two of my routine is to empty all the balls from the basket into the receptacle next to the mat. At this point I give them all a cursory look to ascertain the age and experience of each one. There are important reasons for this. New balls only show up on leap years. Even though they try to disguise old balls by painting them over and over, you can tell they're duds by the pitiful way they try to fly. When I tag one well, it starts out like any ordinary golf ball that should travel 240 yards, but it mysteriously quits dead in midair, 145 yards out. It immediately falls 90 degrees to the earth. I liken the comparison of new versus dud balls to that of a glider and a 747 jumbo jet. Finding brand new balls in a bucket at the range is so rare, they are referred to as "nuggets"—because they sail like gliders. Old, or dud balls dive like a 747 that's just run out of fuel.

When I've separated the nuggets from the duds (if there even are any), I use all the duds to practice my wedges and short irons where the condition of the ball will have the least impact on the outcome of my stroke. Out of the 200 balls in the basket, I save the two nuggets for my driver. This way, I'll at least know how far I'm hitting one of my clubs and I'll have the experience of seeing at least two beauties soar.

Touring pros and instructors tell us that when we practice we should practice for accuracy and distance. It is important to know precisely how far you hit each club, because proper club selection on the course accounts for at least 4 strokes a round. There are, however, two problems with this assumption. First, all balls and ranges are not equal, giving us unclear and inaccurate data. Most ranges recycle balls until they have been pulverized so many times, from so many directions, that, under closer scrutiny, the poor orb is more of a three-dimensional hexagon than a truly balanced sphere. Second, for some unknown reason, most driving ranges face into the wind and sun and go uphill, making it difficult to judge distance or accuracy. We never really know what we're doing until we actually play. Add to this the phenomenon of always being able to swing well at the range and poorly in play, it would seem the deck is stacked against us.

As part of my routine, I've learned to compensate for these problems. If I'm pounding my drives uphill and into a stiff wind, with the scorching sun in my eyes, and I can hit the ball 210 yards, I figure, then under playing conditions, that's a good 240-yard drive.

Part three of my range routine is to locate the right height of the rubber tee. The range owners don't like to spend money on these items either. Usually they are either too long or too short. I finally wised up and bought a bag of my own in 6 different heights.

Now, I'm almost ready to begin. As I watch my fellow addicts, it crosses my mind how each of the stages of my golf journey is represented by one of these guys. Down the line about three mats is the guy who is bending clubs in his teeth. He mumbles four-letter words under his breath after each flailed attempt. That was me 3 years ago. Next to him is a guy taking his lesson, whiffing each shot and topping the ball 3 feet in front of him. He grins sheepishly each time, and his instructor rolls his eyes and says, "That's okay. Just relax and take it real slow." That was me 2 years ago.

Further up the line there is the poser. He's proud as punch of his swing. It takes him 3 hours to hit a single bucket and after each shot he holds his pose for 5 minutes, as if he's being painted by Michelangelo, until his ball comes to a full rest. He savors the moment like a vegetarian who's fallen off the wagon and has just taken his first bite out of a $30 porterhouse. And he knows the precise location of every single ball he's hit. Every once in a while, he'll really tag one that will go out almost to the 220-yard marker on the fly and he'll breathe a slow, contented "Ah, yes!"

Some Fun Ranges for You to Visit

These ranges, a few of the many I've visited, are among the most memorable:

• The Family Golf Center at Chicago Metro

This is one of the most striking driving ranges I've ever seen. Set on 36 acres, it boasts all the amenities you could ever want: a heated range (not the grass), a 9-hole, par-3 course complete with an island green, a patio bar, and more. The television shows *ER* and *Chicago Hope* have both filmed here just to get great shots of the range with the night lights of the skyscrapers along the Loop in the background. Be sure to go at night.

• Golf Club at Chelsea Piers, New York

Open until midnight, this club has 52 hitting stations that feature the same kind of automated teeing machines used at Cracker Jax in Scottsdale. The best part, though, is that it's four stories high and each station is in its own box. When viewed from the range, it looks like a giant version of the television game show *Hollywood Squares.*

• Fox Creek Golf Club, Legacy Golf Links, Smyrna, Georgia

Two properties, side-by-side, form the largest practice facility you've ever seen: 140 stalls and two 18-hole executive courses. The deep bunkers on the courses were troughs used by soldiers to hide in during the Civil War.

• The Islands Golf Center, Anaheim, California

An oasis amidst urban sprawl, this center has greens made of polystyrene "islands" that float in a lake. Otherwise normal golf balls have air injected into their centers so they stay afloat when you miss the greens. They feel like real balls but fly about 10 percent less in distance. A boat with a giant net scoops up all the balls several times a day.

Driving Range Tips

Here are some guidelines for successful range practicing:

- Always, always put the bucket under the opening for the balls of those automated machines before you put the token in.
- Use positive self-talk. This is referred to as "No dog talk." If you must swear, do it quietly so you don't disturb others around you.
- Don't walk too closely behind the golfers as they swing. You could end up with a set of false teeth.
- Always use a specific target for all your shots. This can be the yardage markers or a particular hill or even discoloration in the grass. I always like to see if I can hit the guy who drives the miniature troop carrier they use to scoop up the balls. I figure if I can hit a moving target, I can certainly hit the fairway.
- Buy your own rubber tees in five different heights or hit off the more expensive grass portions of the range, which is actually better for your game anyway.

CHAPTER 14

THE LESSON:
FINDING THE RIGHT THERAPIST

When I was a child my mother forced me to take accordion lessons. I wish she had forced me to take golf lessons instead. I remember having to practice the wind box in the afternoons while all my friends were outside playing ball or having fun getting into trouble. I hated it and so I never became very good, and when I was old enough to say, "I quit," I did.

Now that I reflect back, what was my mother thinking? Right now I could be on the senior tour pulling down a cool $2 to $3 million a year playing sissy golf but, no, she wanted me to take accordion lessons. Did she think I was going to grow up and become rich and famous like what's-his-name on the Lawrence Welk show? How was I going to make a living? Playing bar mitzvahs and gypsy weddings? I don't blame her, though, because now that I think about it, back then Byron Nelson and Sam Snead were winning tournaments left and right, and all they brought home were 5-foot-tall silver chalices and $200.

Much later in life I did take up the piano, realizing that I really did want to play an instrument and play it well. I bring all this up because these experiences are very similar to my approach to golf, which I'll describe momentarily. Like my first endeavor with the accordion, the second at the piano didn't last long either, although I practiced much harder and for longer periods of time.

I remember the day I decided to quit trying. It was when I asked my teacher how long it took the average person to learn to play the piano well enough so as not to embarrass himself in front of his friends. He replied that it would take at least 3 years and could take as long as 5 or 6. Yikes! That's a long time to wait to be the life of the party.

After more than 50 golf lessons and countless hours on the course and the driving range, I see that learning to play the piano well and becoming good at golf both require a remarkably similar devotion. I can clearly see that after 3 years, I will not be embarrassing; after 5, I will be downright entertaining; but for now, I still need lessons and, unlike the accordion and piano, I enjoy practicing golf.

My first lesson was a complete disappointment. I don't know what I was really expecting, but I didn't get it. "Let me see your swing," my instructor said. Instant paralysis. Suddenly fumbling, I began to have a golf-club-choking, sweaty, everyone-at-the-range-stopping-in-mid-swing-to-watch-me seizure. "Okay, that's all right, just relax, take another swing," he said. After about 15 minutes of this I finally settled down and actually hit the ball. Even though I had been playing for 6 months, I had a lot of trouble hitting the ball that day in front of my teacher. Later on I found out, after a particularly miserable day of golf with an important client, that this is called "performance anxiety." It takes place on the golf course only when you are playing with people you want to impress or when you are taking a lesson.

Adding insult to injury, my instructor told me to get another bucket of balls so we could resume my embarrassment. This particular lesson was at a driving range that had automated ball machines, which I had never used. You buy a token at the counter and insert it into the machine to obtain your balls. Still smarting a little from my embarrassing showing at the mat and not thinking clearly, I inserted the coin into the slot without that all-important first step: putting the basket under the opening. One hundred and twenty bouncing balls came pinging and ponging out between the feet of the people who had just moments earlier watched my humiliating swing. Snicker, snicker, snicker. Suddenly I felt like I was right in the middle of an *I Love Lucy* episode. I'm certain, though, that at least one other person on the planet has done the same thing—at least I hope so.

Eventually, I found a great teacher, Keith Behrens, who in many ways was also my therapist. Just when I thought I had finally solved the mysteries of the game, my swing, course management, and the

ability to select clubs would all leave me. Here was my thinking:
Because I didn't start until I was 48—a Methuselah to today's kids
who begin at 3 years old and are playing scratch golf by the age of 8—
I needed to practice longer and more often to catch up. If I wasn't on
that range five times a week, I literally lost all feel for where the club
was or where I was for that matter. I would go into a panic mode and
call Keith for comfort and advice. His advice for my swing was always
the same: "Quit trying to take control. Let your mind go and your body
will follow." Just like life.

How to Swear at Yourself without Disturbing Others around You

"What a blithering idiot! It would help to put the damn basket
under the machine," I muttered to myself. I used to talk to myself a lot,
both on the range and the course. This was not what you would call
positive self-talk. It was a belittling, finger pointing, haranguing-of-me
by me. I'm so smart I don't need anyone to tell me how stupid I am;
I can do it myself. In golf, this is called "dog talk," a verbal or internal
berating of oneself, and it's strictly verboten if you are ever going to
play well.

I've seen plenty of other players talk to themselves in this very
same fashion. "You dummy. You fool. Get your act together, Robert," I
would say to myself. As I was beating myself up verbally, I was
joined on the range by a chorus of dog-talking masochists, all groaning precisely the same things, filled with an equal amount of self-
loathing. In golf, no matter how stupid you've been or how poorly
you've played, you can at least take solace in the fact that many others
have already traveled that path.

I don't talk negatively to myself much anymore. It's very counter-
productive. Your muscles have memory and your brain has total recall
of all that garbage. If you say it often enough it becomes an audio tape

that your brain plays back even before you begin to swing. I've learned to play the patience game. Learning to be patient and positive is not easy, but it leads to a much quieter life-style and far better scores.

I am particularly quiet on the course now because I've found an advantage to keeping mum. Previously, when I hit a bad shot, I knew it the moment the ball flew off the clubface, and I would start screaming and using all sorts of body language to try to coax the ball back to the course. However, there were a few times when the most atrocious shots actually ended up working out quite well. I changed my attitude one day at a course called Pala Mesa in Temecula, California.

Playing and betting with some friends and business associates, I sculled my second shot badly on a difficult par 4. The ball never rose more than 2 inches off the turf as it traveled into a bunker just to the left of the green. As luck would have it, no one was close enough to hear the shot and thus did not realize I had topped it. The ball skated through the sand, hit the lip of the bunker, bounced out, hit a dead tree branch, careened to the right, took a long slow ride down the top tier of the green, and came to rest on the bottom tier—4 inches from the hole! I, of course, gave a slight smile and a nod and proceeded as if nothing unusual had happened. You never know when the golf gods are going to smile on you, so learn to keep your mouth shut.

How to Find the Right Therapist

Actually, you don't find your instructor; he finds you. There isn't a player in the world who wouldn't benefit from lessons with the possible exception of Lee Trevino, who once said, "Before I'd take a lesson from anyone, he'd have to beat me first." Any takers? It is estimated that only 8 percent of all the players in the United States take lessons, so, in order to make a living, most instructors have to resort to some salesmanship.

We begin at the range. Teaching pros call this long row of mats "the line." People who teach there find new customers by "working the line." Sometimes they are very up-front about soliciting business. Typically, an instructor will find a centralized mat on which to hit balls and to display a small sign that says something like, "Professional lessons. Individual or group rates." It will have his or her name and a phone number. This low-key tactic alone rarely generates much interest but the instructor does get to practice a lot. Some instructors have to eventually work the line. When doing so, the typical tactic is to pace slowly up and down behind the mats, eyeing potential customers. If he's a good self-promoter, he won't approach guys who are really bad. That makes for too much work, and the true novice rarely returns often enough to make it worthwhile. Golf instructors, like every businessman, are looking for the repeat customer: the guy who thinks he's pretty good but, in effect, has a flawed swing and is only hitting one out of three well. This is the type of individual who really wants to get better and can afford it. He's probably had some lessons and is firmly hooked on the game.

Once the instructor finds a potential student, he will stand off to the side and just observe for a while, alternating approving nods with the occasional "Tsk! Tsk!" This makes the golfer very self-conscious, and he will begin to hit the ball even worse than before, because he's now focused on the guy watching him and not what he came to practice.

Eventually the instructor will approach this stranger as he's taking a short break, wiping the sweat off his brow and grip. "Can I ask you something?" the instructor will query.

The surprised subject will usually stutter, "Uh, sure, what?"

"Well, I was watching you swing the sticks, and I just thought you had such a nice fluid swing."

"Well, thanks. I've never thought of it as fluid, but I guess it gets the job done," the guy will beam.

Then the instructor will add,"Your swing is so smooth. I'll bet if you pulled your right arm in ever-so-slightly on the down swing, it would be near perfect and you'd get another 25 yards out of each ball."

Our friend is on the hook now, wiggling like a bigmouthed bass. "Do you mind if I show you something that works really well for me?" says the instructor.

"No, sure, go ahead," the fish replies.

Instructors are a little like psychiatrists. When you ask them a question, they don't answer you but just ask you back, "What do *you* think?" In the short time you have, you never feel like you've quite gotten enough information, but you do feel a little better and you think this will translate into better play the next time. Nothing could be further from the truth. Remember, golf is a game of opposites. It's a universal rule of the golf gods that, after you've spent time trying to fix something, the next time you go out and play or practice everything will be out of whack and some other part of your swing will need to be corrected. It's a case of cause and effect. A change in your left arm is going to affect something in your right leg which, in turn, will cause your hips to be out of balance. (The knee bone's connected to the shin bone; the shin bone's connected to the ankle bone; and so on.)

One of the most successful teachers was the fine player, Tommy Armour. He developed a following and reputation as a keen student of the swing. He had a great personality and developed an "attitude" that served him well. As his students flailed away at balls, he would sit quietly, sipping colorful drinks with little umbrellas in them. He charged $50 an hour for lessons, which is amazing considering he was teaching during the depression. It is written that although he gave only a few minutes of hands-on help during a one-hour lesson he was booked for more than 6 months at a time. One of his books, published in 1953, sold an unheard of at the time 400,000 copies.

To be fair to teachers, they are an important element of the game. If you want to play better, it's a good idea to take no less than a lesson a week from a PGA professional and for at least 3 months.

Zen Golf

Michael Murphy, who wrote *Golf in the Kingdom,* also founded Esalon, the self-awareness retreat in central California. If you are old enough to have lived through the '60s, you know what Esalon was.

Now, some 37 years after its real heyday, you can pay to take all your golf inhibitions there and learn how to find inner peace and, just maybe, play golf a little better.

Golf and meditation. That's just how serious all this is. There is a way and place where we can meditate in search of a higher quality of golf. There isn't this much time or thought being spent on a cure for cancer—this is serious stuff!

At Esalon they offer three-day golf clinics, during which participants actually play very little golf. The first thing everyone is taught is how to "let it go," one of the keys to golf's higher planes. The facilitators tell you not to try so hard. Then they line you up with your fellow golf fanatics and have you throw golf clubs at archery targets about 20 yards away. Just throw the club at the target, softly, underhanded, in kind of a gentle, flowing, Esalon kind of way. In this setting, throwing your clubs is symbolic of letting go. On the course, it's more symbolic of a bad game.

Learning Tips

Being a good student of the game is one of the best ways to improve your golf. Here are some great ways to improve:
- Take notes and refer to them often. You'll soon build a library of tips and techniques that will become ingrained in your memory so that every time you're playing a round and you're

about to take a swing, you'll have plenty of swing keys to totally confuse you.

- Play the cheaper courses so that you can play more often. Playing the game is the best way to learn. Look at it this way: the game of golf was meant to be played on courses designed by the gods and nature, complete with ruts, wagon wheel furrows, and concretelike bunkers. You'll learn to be a better player than if you play often on manicured fairways and greens.

- Practice your weaknesses, not your strengths. This, of course, will mean that most of the time you'll be out on the range hammering away with the driver.

- When you're first learning a new swing or technique, it will feel strange and uncomfortable. That doesn't mean it's wrong— it's just that you have been doing it wrong until now. If it continues to feel awkward after two sessions, go back to the drawing board!

- Learn from every mistake. Play with people better than you (which won't be difficult because, until you've been playing about 5 years, everyone will be better than you). Watch, listen, and ask questions. These steps will help to elevate your play.

- Get the Golf Channel on your cable or satellite system and watch it until your wife complains. Then go into another room and watch it some more.

— CHAPTER 15 —

THE IMPORTANCE OF CIGARS AND OTHER GOLF GIZMOS

Cigars have become an essential part of the game, which became obvious when entrepreneurs started selling more than three kinds of cigar holders for use during play. A few of the sillier examples include a stick with a trough at the top to stab into the ground and ever-so-delicately hold your stogie, a hat with an elastic cigar-holding band on the side, and a special gizmo that snaps on your bag to hold your butts.

Why have cigars become an integral part of the game? I have a theory. Although a great many women play golf—and play it quite well—golf is really a little boy's game. Think about it. When a guy plays golf, he gets to pee outdoors behind trees and ride go-carts all around, acting foolishly and bumping them into things and sliding sideways on those fat tires. He gets to whack a ball with a stick, just as he did in a sand lot or on a street corner when he was a kid. He gets to wash his balls in that red up-and-down-brush thingie. And he gets to smoke something he shouldn't, preferably the fatter, longer, and stinkier, the better.

Although cigar smoking has become almost as phenomenally popular as golf, it still carries a taboo in most populated areas. Even the few bars and restaurants that will still allow your cigarette won't allow you to smoke one of those horse legs inside.

Like little boys who enjoy doing things they're not supposed to do golfers think, cigars are an important part of golf. We're really not even supposed to enjoy golf. It's such a useless waste of time chasing a little ball all over the place when there are far better things to do like mowing the lawn, fixing a leaky pipe, going to your wife's favorite charity luncheon, or—gasp—going to church. I've decided golf is my church. Don't get me wrong. I am a believer, but I don't go inside churches much anymore—in fact, not since my last accordion lesson.

Think of it! A church where you can smoke cigars while you commune with Mother Nature and the golf gods. Unlike regular church where you have to cram all your praying in between a few songs in less than an hour, at golf church you can pray and smoke big stinky cigars for 5 hours!

Cigar Etiquette

Now we have to add cigars to our list of golf manners. Let's look at some cigar rules. Even though a cigar can be enjoyed anytime during a round (although a 6:00 A.M. tee-off time is a bit early for me), it's better to wait until your game is warmed up before you light up. Sometime after the 8th or 9th hole seems about right.

Although it is okay to lay your cigar aside on the fairway while you survey and prepare for your next shot and ultimately swing away, it is considered poor taste to leave it on the green when you're about to putt.

Next, you never just discard your cigar butt on the course. This doesn't mean you can use the sand-and-seed box to put it out, either. It's not an ashtray. Nor, does it mean you can throw it into Mulligan Lake, the water dispenser, or smoosh it on the tire of your cart.

It is preferable to douse it out of sight of others in some quiet patch of dirt and then "field strip" it. For those of you who were fortunate enough not to be drafted into the army, field stripping your butts was the law. You pinched out the heat and then peeled back the wrapper slowly and let whatever smidgen of tobacco that was left waft its way about in the wind, as if to make it harmlessly disappear.

It is not polite to smoke alone. Although it isn't necessary to carry extras for strangers, one should always carry enough stogies to accommodate yourself and however many friends you're playing with. This is another little boy rule. You wouldn't walk over to the ice cream store with your best buddy without either knowing he had enough for a cone or that you could afford to buy one for both of you.

Cigars are kind of like ice cream to grown men. They are best savored after a fine meal with a delicate cognac or on the golf course after things are either getting rough or they're going great—you can use either excuse.

When my game is out-of-whack and I've finished nine holes over 46, I'll immediately light one up for good luck. When we reach the 10th hole, I'll announce to everyone, "Well, it's a whole new ball game, a new nine, and I've got my lucky cigar."

Some men walk around all day with their cigars lit and dangling from their lips. They don't need fancy holders. This is a trademark for the long-time PGA professional and now senior tour player, Walter Morgan. Whether he's driving or putting, that man has a perpetual cloud of smoke enveloping his head, from his neck to the tip of his cap; and he seemingly never takes his cigar out of his mouth. As the day wears on, that big slobbery nub is dead, not even a smolder, but it's still hanging there from the corner of his mouth. It must be his lucky cigar.

Golf Gizmos

What is a golf gizmo? It is any little- or medium-sized item we use or play with that we can't remember the name of. Not only have cigars become an important part of the ritual within the game, so have the myriad devices, trinkets, self-help contraptions, and other hard-to-describe objects that we buy and carry with us. If you will remember back a few chapters, where we went through my bag and discovered enough rations for a stay at the North Pole, we can add the following must-have items to our game—some helpful, some suspect, some ridiculous.

All golfers believe in witch doctors. Many on the PGA Tour and several million amateurs have taken to wearing magnets on their bodies when they play the game. In addition, there are the copper wristbands to rid us of our wrist, finger, elbow, shoulder, lower-back, and knee pains. I have to include myself in this group just because of the possible placebo effect of the copper bands. Having worn one now for more than a year to ease my finger and shoulder pain, I can attest that it works. Of course, I always take a half a bottle of aspirin at about the same time I slip it on, so who knows?

As far as magnets go, one of my best golfing buddies wears a girdle-like belt, something akin to what a weightlifter wears for his back. This black nylon belt has about 30 small magnets stitched into it and these are pressed against his lower back when he cinches himself in before each round. He claims it really works. Which reminds me of a story about Ben Franklin. During Ben's heyday, when he was trying to electrocute himself with kites and lightning, magnets were also considered a miracle cure for arthritis, or lumbago, or whatever they called it in those days.

Ben, a wannabe scientist, was naturally skeptical about the wonders of magnets so he conducted one of the first double-blind medical experiments ever. He gave several of his political cronies real magnets for their aches. Then he painted a bunch of rocks with black paint and gave them to a group of his political foes, telling them they were magnets. Guess what? Both groups reported miracle cures from their afflictions and several were felled by lightning. I attribute the results of Ben's experiments to the extraordinary power of our minds to believe and have faith in a cure for our frailties. Faith can work miracles. How else could we possibly continue to play golf?

When I played with the surgeon and the salesman in Sedona, Arizona, the surgeon noticed my copper band and asked me if I thought it really worked. Here was a guy who had probably spent the last 10 years of his life studying medicine, chemistry, biochemistry, neurological physiology, drugs, nuclear biology, and who knows what else, and he's asking me if I think copper wrist bands work! "Most definitely!" I told him. "I notice you are also wearing a copper bracelet." And although I wanted to say "I notice that yours is inlaid with 24-carat gold and two large diamonds with just a smidgen of copper on the underside," I didn't.

He replied that he had indeed worn one for quite some time but noticed that I was wearing mine with the opening down on the bottom of my wrist rather than on top. If you haven't ever seen one of these bands and you play golf, then you are playing on a different planet than I am. They are not a solid band, but rather an incomplete circle that allows about an inch of space so it can be bent slightly and slipped over one's wrist. This makes it cheaper for the manufacturers because one size fits many wrists.

I was to learn yet another valuable golf lesson, or at least, a golf-related lesson. According to the doctor, you are supposed to wear the band with the opening on the top of your wrist if you have upper body pains and on the underside of your wrist if you have lower back or leg pains. "Wow!" I thought, "This voodoo stuff is really sophisticated. It isn't enough that we perceive that copper cures arthritis, we have to elaborate on our superstitions by giving specific spatial powers to it in relationship to its position on our bodies. Hey, as far as I'm concerned, if it doesn't hurt it might work. I'd drop my drawers at the first tee and rub a penny on my butt for an hour, if Arnold Palmer told me it made his pain go away and made him a better golfer."

Gizmo Tips

Here are a few tips that you can use to get the most value out of cigars and other golf gizmos:

- If you're going to smoke a cigar, better bring some extras along for the others. This way, you're being polite and the others won't snicker as much when you hit a bad shot.
- Learn how to field strip your cigars; don't just leave them in the grass when you're done.
- If it works, and it makes the pain go away, use anything you want, including copper bands, magnets or even bagpipes.

CHAPTER 16

THE OBSTACLE COURSE

Let's talk about those conniving people who design golf courses or, as I like to refer to them, obstacle courses. It is important to know how a designer thinks because you aren't just playing against the ball, yourself, and your buddies as you thought. You're fighting the course as well.

Course architects use optical illusions, subterfuge, grass, sand, trees, rocks, rivers, the prevailing weather, lakes, ponds, and whatever else they have to work with or dream up to defend their creations from the likes of you and me.

In the beginning, the greatest course architect was nature. Early links were carved from great swaths of hills and dunes on the coast of Scotland by the golf gods themselves. Once the gods roughed out the basic shape, rabbits, cows, and sheep handled the details. The weather was ferocious; it still is. To protect themselves from the monsoonlike rains that hurled ball-bearing size drops at the landscape, the animals had to hide so they burrowed into the hillsides and dug trenches, otherwise known as "bunkers."

Courses haven't changed much in 300 years. They're meant to beat you into submission or at the very least penalize you severely for making stupid decisions. If you want to find the true essence of the game, play Prestwick, Royal Troon, Turnberry, Carnoustie, or Gullane. You'll be beating balls in a gail from the gorse and heather and then trudging up 40-foot-high dunes lugging your bag (no carts allowed) to each subsequent shot. On these courses, you can play through winter, spring, and fall—all in one day!

Many people—certainly the Scots—feel this is the only way golf should be played. They contend that we Americans have bastardized, diluted, and civilized the game far too much with our manicured fairways, fluffy sand traps (don't let a Scot hear you calling a bunker a sand trap), and greens that are tended by agronomists with Ph.Ds using toenail clippers.

Boot Camp

My home course certainly doesn't fall into the aforementioned category. I call it the obstacle course because it reminds me of my boot camp training in the army. In boot camp, we had to complete a two-mile run over fjords and rivers, through dense thicket shrub, under fallen trees, and around some surprise man-made entrapments, all within a 30-minute time period. On my home course, we have to navigate about 4 miles of treacherous terrain, hacking up sod and circumventing obstacles such as massive bunkers, forests of trees, elephant grass, beer cans, and lakes—all supposedly within 4 hours. Ludicrous!

My course looks more like a World War II battlefield, just after they've hauled off the bodies left from a squadron bombing run. It's complete with potholes, wheel ruts, two-foot-high weeds, gravel where there should be fairway, and bone-dry, hard-pan greens with less grass on them than hair on Michael Jordan's head; but I love it. It's so much like the old Scottish links, where I pretend I'm playing.

For those of you who have never seen or played the old course St. Andrews in Scotland, you're in for a big surprise. That ancient course is rough, tough, and real ugly. There are plenty of bare dirt spots and very little green grass as we know it on the country club courses of America. Fairways aren't always so easy to find and the rough is impossible. There is something very primitive yet charming about it. One recent visitor from America to St. Andrews asked his native-born partner, "Who designed this damned course?" His partner replied, "God."

I figure if I can play well here hitting out of a furrow from behind a discarded Schlitz Malt can, I can play St. Andrews. Playing my home course just makes the rare round at a good $125 course that much more enjoyable. Sometimes the fairways are so groomed and gorgeous on the better courses in comparison to mine, I don't even want to take a divot.

Knowing we are fighting the course as much as the ball, the weather, and our minds, let's take a quick quiz to see how much you know about designers and their creations.

- What are a course designer's three favorite dirty tricks to fool you?
- How can bunkers be friendly?
- What is the invisible hazard on the course?
- What do the mowing patterns over the grass tell you?

No two courses are the same and that is part of the fascination with the game. An ever-changing, divergent landscape to roam, it's meant to both free and challenge your mind. To play well it's good to know how and why designers create these masterpieces. Knowing your enemy's mind-set will come in handy if you're going to be able to analyze the features of the course, including the natural elements, in order to give yourself a fighting chance at breaking 90 or 100.

On a well-designed course, the architect wants each of your shots to contain a risk and reward factor. He feels the course should force you to make countless decisions based on nerve and skill. With my game that decision is easy: every shot is a risk to either my score or a bystander—with precious few rewards.

The Battlefield

It will help if you visualize the course as a battlefield, since you're attacking the course and it, in turn, is trying to defend itself from you. I liken the entire experience to war. In golf, as in war, your attack will consist of strikes by air, land, and sea, trying to weave through the course's defenses by choosing the best takeoff and landing zones.

You should be aware that when a designer sets out to build a new course, the first thing he does is analyze the existing landscape and prevailing weather. From which direction does the wind usually blow? How often does it rain? How can I use the trees and rocks and snakes that are already here to keep these guys from scoring? Why do you think that 458-yard, par-4 at your course plays into the wind?

Choose Your Weapons

One of the best weapons at your disposal is not your 8-iron, it's your scorecard. By taking the time to study the configuration of each hole, where the hazards are, and the distances to them, you can formulate a strategy. Having a scorecard is like getting your hands on the enemy's maps and battle plans. The designer will, for example, try to fool you by placing a row of tall trees behind a green, giving it the illusion that it is closer than it really is. You've got the map in your hand that tells you just how far away that hole is, so don't let your eyes fool you. It's also a good idea to take note of the yardage markers for this same purpose. What else does a scorecard tell you? Just about everything you'll need to know to design your own battle plan.

Take a look at the entire card first and note where the par 5s and 3s are. Although the front and back nine may both be a par 35, that doesn't mean they are equal in difficulty. If there are five par 3s on the course and three of them are on the back nine, you may still have a chance if you had a bad front nine. These extra 3s on the back were probably used to balance the three par 5s on the front, so knowing these kinds of things will help you to get a sense of the rhythm of the entire course. The designer wants to upset your rhythm, so look for sharp swings from very hard to easy and back again.

Also on your card take note of the slope rating. The higher the slope rating—usually between 110 to 150—the harder the course and the more likely you'll need a tourniquet to stop the bleeding. You can give yourself a better chance if you stop being macho and change from the blue to the white tees on a course with a severe slope. Personally, I play the whites on any course that has a rating above 135. At a course in California called Hidden Valley, I played from the blue tees, which had a slope rating of 141. I got an old-fashioned butt-whipping in front of my best friends—on my birthday—no less!

Bentgrass, Bluegrass—It's All Salad to Me

All grass is not equal. Greg Norman knows this perhaps better than anyone. He owns more than 25 sets of clubs and he uses all of them depending upon the type of grass he will be playing on and in what part of the world. Norman knows he needs every edge he can get. If he isn't fighting the fescue, then he's battling the Bermuda; but even more important, he's trying to outwit the course architect, our common arch rival.

You may not be aware of it when you look out at that beautiful expanse of lush green fairway, but even the grass you play on is chosen as an obstacle. The more you know about it, the better your mood will be at the end of the day. A designer chooses a particular grass for two reasons: First, for economic considerations he plants a lawn that will thrive under the local conditions with the least amount of maintenance. Second, he chooses the most difficult grass to play on, that is affordable, especially for the areas of rough. For example, in the northeastern, northwestern and Western United States, bentgrass is primarily used for fairways. It loves the heat and humidity, but more important, it produces a "tight lie," which means a ball doesn't roll very far after it lands. This is a good example of the mind-set of the enemy.

This would be like going to your local bowling alley and finding that the maintenance crew had taken all the grease off the lanes and scuffed them with Brillo pads so they were rough and slow, causing your ball to roll like a cube of wet dough. How long would you continue to bowl there? Golfers are different; we like punishment.

Then there's Bermuda, bluegrass, fescue, kikuyu, rye, and zyosi, each with its own built-in defense mechanisms. Whatever they call it, it's all salad to me. If I'm in the rough, I might as well use a Weedwhacker as any one of my clubs, because I can never extricate myself. Once I'm in it, I stay in it all the way to the green. My home course is a perfect example. Kikuyu grass is used in the rough. When I get into it on any given hole, I feel like a spectator rather than a part of my group. As my partners move down the fairway, I follow along all alone, parallel to them, 40 yards away in the rough, one miserable shot after another, in a futile attempt to reach the green. I never seem to grasp the concept of just taking my lumps and pitching out to the side, losing a stroke but gaining the fairway in the bargain.

As further proof of kikuyu's club-snarling, venus-fly-trap ability to keep you from scoring, during the 1998 Nissan Open held at Riviera, which is known for its kikuyu, they let this nasty stuff grow to about 5 inches long. When the television cameras searched for balls, they couldn't even see the players' shoes! The intention, of course, was to reward the accurate shooters and severely punish those who either tried the shortcuts or just weren't hitting well that day. It worked! Throughout the tournament, everyone complained bitterly.

Understanding how the rough has been cut is vital to escaping it. One trick is to look for cutting patterns left by the mower. Depending upon how devious a greenskeeper wants to be, he can mow it from tee to green or from green to tee. Careful observation will tell you which way it's mowed, and if it is growing toward the tee, it will be growing against you all the way; but you can elect to chip out side-ways into the fairway rather than spending your day in the jungle. There's that risk-and-reward factor again.

Hiding in the Bunkers

In World Wars I and II, bunkers protected the soldiers from enemy gunfire, just as the early links' bunkers protected the animals from the weather. For this reason, bunkers on earlier built courses were found just helter-skelter. It wasn't until the game spread to England that bunkers were created as part of a plan by evil designers. This strategy resulted in hundreds of bunkers being built into courses to be sure they created plenty of trouble along the way. During the Great Depression, however, golf clubs couldn't afford to maintain as many bunkers, so there are fewer now but the ones that are left have been designed with you, the attacking force, in mind.

Bunkers are usually placed where most golfers (meaning intermediate to good) will hit their balls. Here are a few of the bunkers you will encounter on most courses:

- Carry bunkers—These are placed to disrupt your rhythm more than anything else because they are flat and easy to get out of. They're usually well short of your landing area and only there to psych you out. Can you now begin to understand the mind of the designer?

- Collection bunker or a "bath tub"—This is just what it sounds like. It's very deep and is meant to hold things like your ball or an entire squad of infantrymen. These usually have steep front walls forcing you to play out backwards or sideways. Once again, the enemy is using every conceivable defense to keep you from the hole.

- Definition bunker—This type is used as an illusion to fool your perception of depth and make a hole look shorter or longer than it really is, especially on elevated greens. These can be your friends, though, if you use them right. To judge the distance of the green and the position of the pin on an elevated tee with bunkers in front, observe how much of the stick you can see. If you can see most of the pin, you know it's close to a bunker, or closer to the front of the green. If you can't see the pin, it's further back as most bunkers are placed in front or just to the front sides of greens to protect them.

When I first started playing, I avoided the bunkers at all costs. I was scared to death of them and I was quite proud of myself for having seldom found the beaches. However, I learned after awhile that playing out of the sand was actually easier than many of those fringe shots out of the rough grass, so I started honing my sand play. Now I like to proclaim each time I find a bunker, "I love the sand." The pros are so good at hitting out of the soft sand used on PGA courses, they will sometimes hit into a bunker intentionally instead of taking the chance of getting caught in the rough. They know they've got a far better chance of getting up and down.

Still, a bunker well designed for the purpose of creating fear is a hazard to be contended with. The course architect John Low said, "Bunkers, if they are good bunkers, and bunkers of strong character, refuse to be disregarded." Practice your bunker play and save yourself some strokes. And if you're real serious about it and you really want a test, try the 10th hole at Pine Valley Golf Course where the most evil and scurrilous bunker in all of golf resides; it's called "the Devil's Asshole!" There are other bunker types you should become familiar with including pot, saving, waste, and face bunkers.

As in warfare where some people were buried right were they fell, probably in bunkers, there have been some similar stories of burials on the golf course. One that has been circulating for years and could be mythology but is nevertheless entertaining and probably true is about a veteran golfer who spent most of his later days playing cards in the club bar with his pals. He asked that they scatter his ashes over his favorite 12th hole when he died. When he finally did go, his friends, wanting to honor his wishes, took his urn out to the 12th fairway. As requested, they all stood by as his ashes were poured carefully over the lush fairway. As they bade a last farewell and turned to leave, a gust of wind came up and blew him into a bunker, an ironic final note probably exacted by the golf gods for not raking one too many bunkers. Some days, nothing goes right on the course.

Another story—one that has been documented—concerns William Garner who also told his friends to bury him on his favorite hole, the 17th at Croham Hurst Golf Club. At the age of 76, Garner passed on and his friends, honoring his wishes, took his ashes out to the 17th. But instead of spreading him on the fairway, as one final prank of their own, they scattered him over the rough off to the right side where they said that he had spent most of his time.

There are many other ways designers try to fool you. One is by placing tee boxes in areas protected by trees so you won't be aware of the swirling winds on that fairway, and another is by building greens in hilly terrain so they give the impression they are running uphill, when in fact they are actually cantilevered downhill.

Turf Tips

These are but a few of the tactics designers employ but there are ways to even the odds between you and the enemy:

- Read a good book on golf course design and find out how designers create obstacle courses for you. I suggest Robert Trent Jones's book *Golf by Design.*
- Play a course often enough to understand the geography and subterfuge. This is the reason most club members play a course better than you if it's your first few times out.
- Instead of fruitlessly trying to hack forward in the rough, just take your lumps and pitch out to the fairway. Ultimately, you'll save at least 2 strokes.
- Read your scorecard carefully; it's your strongest weapon in the battle.

CHAPTER 17

DRESSING FOR SUCCESS ON THE COURSE

When it comes to fashion, the game of golf rivals Las Vegas for the truly tasteless. When I'm in Las Vegas, I see celebrities coming out of boxing matches dressed like refugees from a Czechoslovakian circus. These are people who normally wouldn't wear anything but Armani and Donna Karan who all of a sudden lose their fashion minds.

Just because they're in the official national adult playground, they think that lime green and fuchsia satin looks great with fur-trimmed hats, sparkles, glitter, and feathers. Suddenly patent leather shirts look appropriate. I tend to dress wild too. I wear funny Hawaiian shirts with tight jeans, a big flashy cowboy buckle, and silly loafers with tassels.

Golf is like that or at least the way the game is played on municipal courses. It has a strange effect on people's fashion consciousness. For some reason, when we go out to play at a nice course or a country club, we want to dress up in a costume too. Look at Payne Stewart. He has either been reincarnated from the 1700s, or he's just plain having fun. Maybe both. Why not?

What better place to be color uncoordinated? We're already that way physically when we play the game. In Las Vegas it's okay to look like a pimp or a peacock, and in golf it's okay to look like your grandma's sofa. If you're going to get dressed up though, why not go all the way? Put on a wig and a skirt and play the women's tee; it's the quickest way to add 60 yards to your drives.

Golf fashion used to be simple. There were rich people, primarily white men, who belonged to expensive country clubs that only welcomed people like themselves. Then there were the rest of us who wore T-shirts and sneakers and played the municipal courses. Now there are three levels of fashion in the sport: First, there is the country club set with their $185 Ashworth shirts and their monogrammed golf bags. This is the Neiman Marcus set.

Second, there are the really nice public courses, which are almost like country clubs but buy-in is only $300 a year instead of a $100,000 membership fee and monthly dues of $1,500. The clothes here aren't always Izod or Ashworth, but they are nice and generally the colors are coordinated. This is the Macy's set.

Finally, there is the municipal course group. These are the people—the biggest proportion of golfers—who play public courses where fees are $18 to $40 plus a cart. Here, just about everybody makes Mr. Blackwell's worst dressed list on a weekly basis. This is the Target and K-Mart set: green and orange plaids, polka dots mixed with stripes, sweaty old ball caps and T-shirts, and sometimes no socks at all—or even shoes.

When I first started playing, I only wanted to play the "nice" courses. I couldn't stand the thought of playing on the rough-hewn city courses with all their dried-up grass, lousy greens, and bare spots. However, as I got better and played more often, I realized two things: first, it's too expensive to pay $125 every time I play, and second, I've discovered the joys of the municipal courses (or munis). I enjoy playing the munis. They're cheap, and I can wear old shorts and my favorite T-shirt and feel completely at ease.

If you play at a country club or the nicer public courses that run in the $100- to $200-a-round range, you know there is a dress code. The codes are very specific: No tank tops or T-shirts and you must have collars on your shirt. Even the length of your shorts is in the code. There is a magic length that is correct for a golf short. I know what it is visually but could not describe it in terms of inches. It falls somewhere between just-above-the knee by about a half-inch, up to about 2 inches above the knee. As you get much shorter, you're not wearing golf shorts; you're wearing something that has yet to be named. With the munis, the dress code is generally that you just have to have something on.

Because more and more younger players are taking up the game and because there is a lot of money to be made in clothing designs and manufacturing, today's golfers are much more hip.

Years ago, shirts were snug and collars were stiff with long tabs and made out of polyester, kind of like the ones John Travolta wore in *Saturday Night Fever.* Golf is a game of tradition so the Old Guard resisted soft collars. Eventually though, comfort and style won out. Now, for the most part, everyone's socks match.

Although golf clothes have become more hip, the USGA hasn't. It still requires professional players to wear long pants even if they're playing a tournament in Palm Springs in August and the temperature is 120 degrees. Apparently the PGA Tour feels the need to preserve golf's status as a gentlemen's game. This didn't bother Mark Wiebe. At a 1992 tournament at Kingsmill Golf Club in Williamsburg, Virginia, after the temperature went over 102 degrees, Mark changed into shorts. He was promptly fined $500.

The long-leg pants rule, however, does not apply to female professionals who routinely wear shorts. I guess this rule is in force to keep us from having to look at the awful sight of knobby-kneed guys with black horse-haired legs in high black socks and Bermuda shorts playing the game we love. On the other hand, since most of the ladies don't have hairy legs, or at least not during the tournaments, it's okay for them to wear shorts.

How to Tell the Good Players from the Bad by Observing Their Clothes and Equipment

There's more to the whole fashion scene in golf than just clothes. Nearly everything a golfer carries with him or wears makes a statement about his ego, fashion sense, and level of experience.

You can almost tell how good or bad a player is by observing his clothes and equipment. A really good golfer rarely has a spanking new bag. Usually his bag is so old and worn out it wouldn't stand up on its own if you took the clubs out of it. A really good player would never put funny animal-head covers on his woods or those silly rubber covers on his irons; after all, they are clubs! The less experienced golfer who has recently purchased his clubs wants them to look nice more than be functional, so he keeps them covered.

Observation has taught me that the more plastic resort tags there are on a player's bag, the bigger his ego. Some guys can't even get into the pockets of their bags because they have 43 of those commemorative tags that have the names and logos of only very expensive golf resorts on them, showing us that they have the time, money, and good taste to play five-star resorts. This is also meant to demonstrate that they have played quite a few rounds.

Hats are symbolic, too. The better players don't wear hats often and, if they do, they generally are sweat-stained limp old cotton baseball caps with a logo that says, "Hank's Diner." Why does everyone wear baseball caps to play golf anyway? Because most of the pros wear them, but then again they're getting paid to. For some unknown reason, women always look cute in baseball caps and men look like idiots. I have a collection of more than 25 baseball caps from various courses around the country and only one of them looks decent on me.

I overheard a conversation a few months ago in the clubhouse where two women were discussing how rude they thought a gentleman at another table was for wearing his hat inside. What they didn't understand is that once you put a ball cap on, you have to leave it on until you go to bed because when you take it off, you will have the dreaded "hat hair." The poor guy had no choice.

Today's "in" fashion accessory for male golfers is short socks. These are the ones that only rise about 2 inches above your tassels. The women golfers have worn them forever but now any male golfer under the age of 65 that wears long white socks is fashion unconscious. I admit it, I wear them, too, but when I take them off and the rest of my body is deeply tanned down to a point 2 inches above my ankles, I look like a guy who survived one of those Mafia hits where they give you concrete shoes and throw you off a pier.

Copper bracelets are a fashion item as well as a pain killer. What used to be a simple flat piece of copper has now been styled with gold and silver with twisted cord in the center and gold knobs on the end so that they can be worn at dinner.

Shoes are definitely a fashion statement and again, with the better players, shoes tend to be more weary than those of the newer players for obvious reasons. And what are those tassels all about? A big flat splayed-out piece of leather that has to be laced over your laces. It's just one more thing to do. Are tassels supposed to be functional? If so, what do they do? Protect your shoe laces? Why are all golf shoes either one solid color, generally black or white oxfords with brown, black, or burgundy sides and heels? We are just now, after more than three centuries of golf, beginning to see Nike and others come out with better looking shoes. The newest trend is to wear the soft-spiked or rubber-ribbed soled shoes with slacks, even in public. The oddest footwear I've seen on the course was when I played in Texas and one of our foursome wore cowboy boots. On the other side of the fashion spectrum, I played with a gentleman in San Clemente, California, who played barefoot. He claimed that not having the traction of his shoes to depend on helped him concentrate on his upper-body turn. After watching him play, I claimed it was the only way he could keep his score on each hole, because he didn't have enough digits on his hands to add up his score.

Probably the best-dressed golfer ever was Walter Hagen who once said, "I don't want to be a millionaire. I just want to live like one." Mr. Hagen, also known as "Sir Walter" or "The Haig," lived the role of a Hollywood star. One of the first to pay much attention to golf clothing at all, he wore alpaca sweaters, silk shirts, loud cravats, cacophonous argyle socks, and his patented black-and-white, $100-a-pair shoes.

Hagen was a striking figure with jet black hair slicked tight on his head, always far ahead of his fashion time. He traveled in chauffeured limousines and golfed with emperors and princes and was known to consume vast amounts of scotch. Hagen probably enjoyed dressing up as much as he loved playing golf. The game gave him a reason to create his own costumes and persona. It seems to me that a lot of the game's earlier players had a flair for fashion, fun, and life in general that isn't seen as much today. Maybe that's because the stakes are so much higher now, making the game far more serious.

Fashion Tips

Heed these fashion "don'ts" before your next trip to the links:

- Don't wear your hat backward. It looks dumb and you'll get a sunburn.
- Don't, under any circumstances, ever wear polyester pants or shirts that were made before 1980.
- Don't wear those stretchy pants with the clamps on the side that allow you to grow 4 inches of extra waist without having to let them out.
- Never, ever, wear black socks with shorts.
- Do not wear patent leather shoes.

— CHAPTER 18 —

THE 19TH HOLE

Many players think that a round of golf ends at the 18th green with the shaking of hands and saying goodbye—thankful the whole miserable mess is over and the bleeding has stopped. Well, the bleeding has, but the bull hasn't. The bar or the clubhouse, commonly referred to as the 19th hole, is where we end the day. This is where tall tales, scores, lies, and excuses are shared; mostly excuses and lies.

This is where we add up our scores and relive each shot and hole vividly. How did the round go? Where did we go wrong? What were the highlights? Were there any highlights?

Here is an excerpt from my 19th hole conversation after the last round of golf I played before turning this manuscript over to my publisher:

> "Hey Ricky! You should have your face on a Wheaties box, that was a great round," I chirp. "Nah, shot a 79 on this cheesy course, shoulda been a 73." (No score is ever good enough for any player who shoots under 80 consistently.) Next to dropping a third testicle, I'd die for his round. As the four of us settle in with a round of drinks and begin to add up our cards, the subject of our inability to drive today comes up.
>
> "Man, I used to be able to drive the ball like a bullet out there 275 yards sweet as you please every time," complains Ralph. "That's because you're old. You

know the saying, "The older you get, the longer you used to be." I've been playing with you since you were 23 years old, and you never hit a ball past 175 yards," reminds Ricky.

"Ralph, your handicap *is* golf. Ya know, they've invented just about every drug we old farts over 50 need: Pills to grow our hair, balms to hide our wrinkles, and then there's that Viagra.

"Too bad they don't have Viagra for your golf game. Might make your putter work better," adds Richard.

"Man, I think I had a brain burp on that last putt. Four inches away and I jerk it to the left. Why do I keep making the same mistakes over and over and over again?" whines Terry. We all have an answer or opinion and so the conversation turns to a more serious analysis of the mistakes we all continually make, calculating out loud how many strokes we all could be shaving off our scores by merely making a few decisions better.

"I could shoot 80 every time out if I could just remember to quit hitting out of trouble into more trouble," Terry says. "Ya know what kills me on these courses where we can't take the cart off the path? I get out there 300 yards away from the cart path and I have the wrong club. Do I run all the way back, or just use what I've got? I could take 3 strokes off each round and I'd be shooting 85 every time," ventures Shawn.

On and on it goes as we think of all the things we continue to do even though we know we shouldn't: hitting away when we know we should back off and regroup mentally, making the last swing thought a negative one, hitting lay up shots too far, and carelessly putting out in a rush to get out of someone's line. Add a few rimmed putts that should've fallen, and we'd be shooting in the low 80s, we all agree.

As all my friends are moaning, laughing, and giving each other verbal jabs, I add up my score and head for the bathroom. Along the way I'm thinking to myself, "Shot an 89 on a tough course today. Could've had an 82. I know exactly where I lost those 6 shots. That 3-putt green on that chintzy par 3—there's one. That lost ball right off the fairway on the 12th, I swear that s.o.b. landed right out in front of that tree—there are 2 more. A chili-dip I did just 15 feet out for a birdie on the 14th that turned into a double bogey—that's 2 more. And that last putt on the 18th that stopped a chest hair from the hole—there's 6." Then, as I turned to go back to the bar, I grow more positive as I think to myself, "Robert, there you go again, dog talking. Take a look at the bright side. Life could be a lot more difficult. This is your meditation. Golf is hope personified. You will never have your best game but you will enjoy more great days like today."

I begin to think about the golf gods once again and remember a legend I once heard about a poor old soul named Mac. He played miserably but his story had a happy ending. This is Mac's story:

The Legend of a Golf God

Mac was a Scot whose swing was so poor,
In a fit he dug a deep channel.
His temper would flair,
And his club would whiff air,
His play gave a bad name to flannel.

Then one lucky day,
After a pitiful drive,
The golf gods exclaimed, "ats enoof."
The sun was to set and note his worst score,
But a golf legend was made with this duff.

Mac's ball came to rest
At the edge of a river,
It looked like an unplayable lie.
His threesome scolding,
"Where it lay ye must play,"
Mac cursed the gods and asked, "Why?"

He dropped to his knees
In a desperate appeal,
"Please, gods, have pity on me."
When he rose to his feet,
In the hopes they had heard him,
He realized they'd answered his plea.

A bright beam of light,
From an oddly shaped stone,
Caught old Mac right in the eye.
Picking it up and rubbing it thrice,
It shone like a star in the sky.

Without hesitation,
He fetched his best stick,
Drew back a deep breath, and envisioned.
The club met the ball with a passionate kiss,
And it rose with angelic precision.

Finding its way from the bed of the river,
His ball landed sweet and true.
As it hit the green and spun back with a vigor,
To the cup it did roll and fall through.

They say that his swing became smooth as fine malt,
He'd hit eagles for scores in the twenties,
As with him each round he carried the wee stone,
Which he rubbed and polished aplenty.

On the day that he died,
While on the backside,
Mac spoke his last earthly advice:

"No golfer should hack,
Nor take any gimmies,
Let him n'er hook, chunk it or slice.

If he's hacking the sod,
And his game's gone to the devil,
Let him find the wee stone and pray,

Golf gods be with me,
Give me big drives and one-putts,
Let me swing like the angels all day.

Remind me I'm human,
I'm meant to have fun,
A bad round's not the worst kind of a day.

The more that I laugh,
And rub me wee stone,
The better and better I'll play."

Those last two stanzas sum up my new understanding of the game:
Remind me I'm human,
I'm meant to have fun,
A bad round's not the worst kind of a day.

The more that I laugh . . .
The better and better I'll play.

When I remember back to the day I broke my hand on the ball-washing machine, I realize my temperament has changed for the better and so has my game. First, the more that I laugh, the better I play. Second, luck plays a role in every round, so it doesn't hurt to pray to the golf gods once in a while. Third, I do a reality check every so often. I've learned not to expect to play like a pro.

As I turned the corner to rejoin my friends in the bar, I thought, "I wouldn't admit it to these guys, but I sure enjoy their company. God, I love this game."

Glossary of Buzzwords and Phrases

Ace—A hole-in-one. Don't concern yourself with it, as your chances of getting one are slim.

Air shot—Not making contact with the ball. The same as a whiff.

Albatross—Three under par or a double eagle. Don't worry about it; it's unlikely that you'll get one of these. The term obviously applies to a par 5 and above; on a par 4 an albatross would be a hole-in-one, which sounds a lot better.

American ball—As agreed by the PGA, 1.68 inches in diameter.

Apron—The narrow zone of short grass surrounding a putting green. The turf here is not as short as on the green and not as long as the fairway grass.

Baffing-spoon—Archaic club used like today's wedges for short, lofted shots.

Bail out—Rescuing a poor tee shot with a great second or third shot or a putt. Also referred to as recovery, which accounts for most of the game.

Banana ball—Shots going to the right, for right-handed players, in a long sweeping arch resembling a banana peel. Also known as a slice.

Beach—A sand trap. Also known as a bunker or the Sahara.

Bermuda—Grass named after the island and used in warmer climates.

Birdie—One under par, it implies that the ball flew like a bird.

Bite—Something yelled often on the course by players wishing for their balls to drop quickly rather than race off into the distance. Usually used on approach shots to the green.

Blade—Hitting the ball across the top with the edge of the club rather than the face. Same as sculling or topping.

Blast—Both a really good day of golf (i.e., having a blast) and to explode out of a bunker.

Blaster—A sand wedge or a driver.

Blow-up hole—A hole where the golfer hits quite a few strokes over par and ruins an otherwise good round. A blow-up hole is known to cause golf rage.

Bogey—One over par. Considered the standard score that a good amateur should be able to make.

Brassie or brassy—An alternate for a number 2-wood. The name given to various lofted wooden clubs in the late 19th century, more than a driver and less than a spoon.

British ball—Smaller and lighter than its American cousin. Not more than 1.62 inches in diameter.

Bunker—A sand trap, the beach, the desert, the Sahara.

Buzzard—A double bogey or 2 over par. A continuation on the theme of birds, i.e. birdie.

Caddie or caddy—Someone who carries a golfer's bag. From several origins, including the French cadet.

Chili-dip—To hit the ground before the ball. Refers to the scooping motion of picking up some chili dip.

Choke—To suffer an onset of nervousness while playing. Refers to the psychosomatic evaporation of saliva and inability to swallow, sometimes leading to actual spasms.

Chunk-it—A chili-dip in the rough. A weak little shot where the ball travels less than a foot.

Cleek—Alternate name for No. 1-iron. Any of the various narrow-bladed iron clubs. From the Scottish clee, hook, crook, a walking stick with a hook.

Calamity Jane—A putter used by Robert Trent Jones, Jr. A hickory-shafted blade putter.

Chinese hook—A ball that travels perpendicular to its intended path. Another term for the shanks.

Cross bunker—An elongated sand trap that runs across a fairway.

Deuce—A hole-in-two. Don't concern yourself as you probably won't see many of these either.

Divot—A piece of turf lifted up by the club.

Dub—Someone unskilled or inexperienced.

Duck—A ball that suddenly dives downward.

Duck hook—A shot that dives down hard and spins left. Uglier than a duck or a hook by themselves, this shot exhibits the worst of both.

Duff—Hitting the ground, then hitting a glancing blow across the top of the ball. Combines the worst of a chunk and a skull.

Duffer—One who continually duffs the ball.

Dunch—Jabbing at the ball without a full backswing.

Eagle—Two under par. Don't concern yourself; you won't see many of these either.

Fairway—That very thin slice of good short grass that runs between the rough on every hole.

Fat—To take more earth than ball, i.e., hitting it fat.

Fescue—A gnarly, insidious weed that passes for grass. Used in rough areas.

Floater—A ball that floats in water. No longer used because the ball-diving companies lobbied for their extinction.

Foozle—A badly hit shot.

Fore—Most widely used four-letter word in golf. Yelled to warn others of your ball's imminent arrival.

Fried egg—A ball that's almost completed buried in sand.

Frog hair—Another term for the apron around a green. Short grass.

Gimmie—Conceding a putt whose distance is so short as to be a "given." Cheating.

Gobble—A hard-hit putt that still manages to find the hole.

Golf lawyer—A player who carries a rule book in his shirt pocket and checks it frequently to insure that everyone is playing properly.

Golfiana—Matters, literature, or artifacts belonging to golf.

Gorse—A spiny evergreen shrub, chiefly British. Very tough rough. Known as Furze in the United States and Whin in Scotland.

Greenskeeper—Contentious and grumpy individual who is responsible for maintenance and management of the course. Intensely dislikes golfers who ruin his turf.

Hacker—One who attacks the ball and plays badly.

Hand wedge—Similar to the foot wedge, only generally used in hidden bunkers rather than out in the open. Also a much easier "club" to use than the foot wedge, which is usually covered by a leather shoe, making impact unpredictable.

Hog's back—A ridge of ground, or a hole having a ridge of ground on the fairway.

Hole—A cylinder 4-1/4 inches in diameter and at least 6 inches deep. The ball's garage.

Honor—The privilege to tee off first on a hole, awarded to the golfer with the lowest score on the previous hole. Not always an advantage.

Hook—For a right-handed player, a ball that bends dramatically to the left.

Jerk—To hit the ball from the rough, sand, or a bad lie with a downward cut. Also, the guy you got paired with who wants to tell you his whole life story while you play.

Jigger—A short club used for chipping; not in use today.

Kick—An erratic, unpredictable bounce sometimes good, sometimes not so good.

Lie—Where your ball comes to rest. What you tell everybody your handicap is.

Marshal—A golf cop. Official originally appointed only to control the gallery; now he tries to control everything.

Mashie—A lofted iron club, no longer in use. Introduced in 1880 and used for pitching with great backspin, almost like mashing the ball with a steep and violent slam.

Nassau—A three-part bet on a round of golf in which an equal stake is wagered on the first nine, the last nine, and on the whole round.

Niblick—A short-headed, steeply lofted wooden club that is no longer in use. Used for playing out of ruts and tight lies; probably the precursor to today's shallow-faced fairway woods. The origin is Scottish, literally meaning "short nose."

Nugget—A brand new ball in a basket full of duds at the driving range.

Outside agency—Any object—including people, livestock, birds, or other animate objects—that stops, deflects, or steals the ball.

Quail high—A shot hit on a low and flattish trajectory. More than likely, most of your drives.

Rabbit—An amateur golfer of little accomplishment or a touring pro who has won no exemptions and must compete in qualifying rounds for a chance to play in a tournament.

Relief—How you feel when a miserable round is over. Permission under the rules to lift and drop the ball, generally without penalty.

Road hole—The 17th hole at St. Andrews, commonly considered the hardest hole in golf.

Royal and ancient—The Royal and Ancient Golf Club of St. Andrews in Scotland. Entitled by permission of King William IV in 1834, in recognition of the fact that golf had then been played in Scotland continuously for about 400 years and that among its devotees were kings and queens of Scotland from James IV onward.

Rutting iron—A club used for hitting the ball out of ruts made by cartwheels.

Sandy—Making par after being in a bunker.

Shanks—A virus of unknown origin that makes the golfer hit the ball perpendicular to its intended path. The afflicted will immediately become sweaty and nauseous.

Scrambler—A player who is erratic but manages to achieve good results through bold recovery.

Tee—Originally a heap of sand used to elevate the ball for driving, it is now any of various reusable or disposable devices on which a ball is placed for driving.

Texas wedge—Attributed to Ben Hogan, who used the term to define a shot made with the putter from outside the green.

Waggle—A warm-up or loosening motion made prior to taking a full backswing.

Worm burner—A low-flying shot; miss hit.